W9-DCL-319

MONTGOMERY COLLEGE LIBRARY
ROCKVILLE CAMPUS

THE ENGLISH STAGE
1850—1950

A LONDON GALLERY IN THE SEVENTIES

Saturday Night at the Victoria Theatre

Fr.

THE ENGLISH STAGE
1850—1950

by

LYNTON HUDSON

GREENWOOD PRESS, PUBLISHERS
WESTPORT, CONNECTICUT

The Library of Congress has catalogued this publication as follows:

Library of Congress Cataloging in Publication Data

Hudson, Lynton Alfred, 1886–
  The English stage, 1850-1950.

  Reprint of the 1951 ed.
  1. Theater--Great Britain--History. I. Title.
[PN2594.H75 1972]   792'.0942   72-6184
ISBN 0-8371-6487-7

Copyright

All rights reserved

First published in 1951
by George G. Harrap & Co. Ltd. London

Reprinted with the permission
of George G. Harrap & Co. Ltd.

First Greenwood Reprinting 1972

Library of Congress Catalogue Card Number 72-6184

ISBN 0-8371-6487-7

Printed in the United States of America

ACKNOWLEDGMENTS

FOR permission to quote from copyright material the author and publishers offer their grateful thanks to the following:

Messrs Chatto and Windus for the extract from *Dramatic Values*, by C. E. Montague.

Messrs Faber and Faber, Ltd, for the extract from *East Coker*, from *Four Quartets*, by T. S. Eliot.

Mrs Frieda Lawrence and Messrs William Heinemann, Ltd, for the extract from the poem *Energetic Women*, from *Poems*, by D. H. Lawrence.

The author would also like to acknowledge the courteous help given to him by the staff of the Enthoven Collection in the Victoria and Albert Museum.

CONTENTS

ILLUSTRATIONS

BY WAY OF INTRODUCTION

"THE Drama," wrote Ellen Terry in a message to the Theatre Conference at Stratford-on-Avon in 1919, "is the child of the theatre. It goes to my heart that the child should be brought up to despise its parent." There has always been a tendency for this to happen. In consequence writers about the theatre have been inclined to concern themselves almost exclusively with the dramatists and to restrict their interest to authors whose work has a literary quality. In so doing they have been careful not to omit some appreciation of poets whose flights of fancy in the theatre have attracted only a highbrow and esoteric audience—yet they have ignored those less literary plays which found favour with the multitude merely because they were 'good theatre.'

But the history of the English stage is not told by the catalogue of its major dramatists. There have been periods when the dramatist has counted for very little; yet the theatre has continued and advanced. Print, however, has made him the least ephemeral, as he is perhaps on the whole the principal factor in the business. But there are other factors: the actor, the producer, even the scenic artist, the critic, and the theorist, who have each in turn had their moment of predominance in the evolution of the theatre and in the education of that other factor, as indispensable to the theatre as the ocean is to a ship, the play-going public. A superficial survey of the history of the English stage gives the impression that *plus ça change, plus c'est la même chose.*

At almost any period you will find the pessimist proclaiming that the drama (like the country) is going to the dogs, while at the same time the optimist is able to discover hopeful signs of its vitality. You will find a condemnation of the commercialism of managers alongside a disinterested and idealistic effort to promote a better theatre. There has been a continuous lament that the art of acting is declining while the actor has steadily risen in prestige. And the public is always being blamed for the depravity of its taste when it simultaneously infuriates authors, managers, and actors by booing rubbish. Yet the theatre has evolved, and in its evolution all these factors have played their part.

It is in order to try to discover how they have each made their contribution that this book has been written. Professor G. M. Trevelyan defined social history as history without the politics. In a sense this is a history of the theatre without the drama. The drama cannot, naturally, be left out. But the dramatists have been so often and so amply evaluated by many competent writers that I have tried to avoid giving them more than their due and necessary importance in this attempt to follow the story of the English stage through the last century. This may have led to regrettable omissions, but this is not a history of the drama, it is rather a scrap-book of those 'unconsidered trifles' which have helped to shape that history: an Autolycan excursion into the stageland of a century.

I

THE TWILIGHT OF THE DRAMA

The Eighteen-fifties

THE curtain rises, as at the beginning of Edmond Rostand's *Cyrano de Bergerac*, on a scene of semi-darkness and confusion. Even to find one's bearings in the motley world of entertainment of the 'fifties it not easy; much less to classify it tidily. To the historian of the drama this semi-darkness is not twilight but inspissate gloom, a night as black, as far removed from culture, as the interior of the dark continent which Dr Livingstone was soon to penetrate. Whereas in every field of literature there was evidence of endeavour, conspicuous and increasing, after correctness, grace, and if possible distinction, the drama had forfeited its right to be considered as literature or even as an art. In consequence the contemporary critic disdainfully ignored it, and the dramatic historian merely accords a brief contemptuous mention to its deplorable eclipse.

It is therefore clearly useless to re-examine the theatre of the eighteen-fifties from an academic standpoint—if, indeed, this is the right approach to the theatre of any period. The playwrights of the time had no literary pretensions. Nor was it by an alliance with English letters that the Victorian theatre survived. It survived by the ill-paid work of hack-playwrights, botchers and plagiarists, whose only talents were the knacks of constructing a theatrically effective situation and of writing emotional rhetoric for artificial characters; it survived through the medium of actors who learned their business the hard way from the Protean drudgery of provincial circuits and stock companies, playing perhaps as many as two hundred different parts in a year, the rank and file barely making a living out of their despised profession, the big names earning perhaps a hundred pounds a week. It survived at the expense of frequently bankrupt managers who were forced to please a public that demanded quantity, not quality, and had to rely on the Christmas pantomime season in order to balance their budgets at all.

The theatre had to contend against religious prejudice and social ostracism, against the competition of opera and ballet, to say nothing of countless respectable and disreputable hybrid forms of rival entertainment. In the boom summer of 1851, the Great Exhibition year, when London was full of visitors, there were nineteen quasi-legitimate theatres open, excluding the two Opera Houses and the St James's, where the Bond Street bookseller Mr Mitchell had provided a permanent home for French actors in a repertory of French classics. During these summer months the theatres were crowded despite the counter-attractions of various dioramas, hippodromes, gardens, casinos, Grecian saloons, and "the innumerable irregulars which swarmed in every corner of the city and the suburbs, and where dramatic performances under some form or other were presented daily and nightly." At Vauxhall Gardens visitors had the thrill of witnessing a balloon ascend to the daring height of 21,000 feet. At the more fashionable Cremorne Gardens patrons could listen to music and eat ices under the trees and watch Madame Antonia, an American lady, perform extraordinary feats upon the tight-rope, ascending to a height of a hundred feet amid a shower of fireworks. As for the saloons, to quote a punning burlesque jingle of the times:

A CHARLES KEAN PRODUCTION

The entry of Bolingbroke into London—a scene from *Richard II*,
at the Princess's Theatre

HORRID REALISM!
An old poster dated 1865

The Drama here one consolation sees—
Her audience may sup porter, if they please.

A very popular entertainment was the Hippodrama, a
novel kind of production in which the principal actors were
horses. More than one successful author was glad to invent
plots for these equestrian performers. In 1853 even the
great national theatre of Drury Lane was turned into a
circus.

Lest they should be accumulating more dust
The boards of Drury Lane are cut for sawdust,
And as the stage won't draw itself perforce is
Dragged through the mire by a strong team of horses.

These lines from Francis Talfourd's burlesque *Alcestis: the
Original Strong-minded Woman* of the same year tersely depicts
the straits of the legitimate theatre. In normal times—except
during the pantomime season, which was growing more
popular every year—managers were hard put to it to fill
their theatres. The privileged theatres had first ceased to
make a living out of their privilege, and then died of it.
Even the veteran Macready, with the support of Bulwer
Lytton and the leading men of letters of the day, had failed
to save them. Drury Lane was delivered over to the
management of an ex-policeman, the egregious E. T.
(nicknamed "Everlasting Testimonial") Smith, who en-
deavoured to entice the public back to that historic playhouse by advertisements crammed with superlatives and
grammatical absurdities puffing the attractions of his
"monstrous productions and gorgeous shows aided by
horses and wild animals." The memory of Garrick and
Mrs Siddons was outraged by the roaring of Van Amburgh's
trained lions. The other privileged theatre, Covent Garden,
was burnt to the ground after a *bal masqué* on March 6, 1856.
Meanwhile the numerous unprivileged theatres which
had been springing up around the two patent houses existed

by evasions of the law forbidding the presentation of "legitimate drama" at any but the two privileged theatres. They loaded their plays with songs and dances, and made out that they were not plays at all. They were also infringing the law by selling tickets for money, but in the early days of the Strand Theatre a way out was discovered for this too. Purchases made at an adjoining confectioner's shop could be exchanged for seats: one ounce of lozenges (4s.) for a box, and one ounce of peppermints (2s.) for the pit. The theatre was nevertheless closed by the Lord Chamberlain, and the actors were fined. These theatres drew rowdy, ill-mannered, and vociferous audiences who clamoured for freaks and acrobats, and for a programme of six or even eight attractions. The passing of the Theatre Act of 1843, removing the restrictions on these unprivileged theatres, had no immediate effect on this class of entertainment. It could not become effective until its new public, the first wave of industrial democracy, had first been disciplined and educated. Charles Dickens, in a letter written in 1851, thus described his recollection of the audience at Sadler's Wells in 1844, when Samuel Phelps began his management there: "As ruffianly an audience as London could shake together. . . . It was a bear-garden, resounding with foul language, oaths, cat-calls, shrieks, yells, blasphemy, obscenity: a truly diabolical clamour. Fights took place anywhere at any period of the performance." At this time also the frequentation of the theatre by loose women had grown to be so flagrant a scandal that it had—vide *The Spectator*—become "an ancillary to the bagnio."

When such conditions prevailed it is not surprising that the *habitué*, the playgoer of the old school, had been driven from the playhouse and that the middle and wealthier classes stayed away from it. There were, of course, other reasons for the decline in theatre-going among the upper classes besides the unpleasantness and physical discomfort of the playhouses—the bad ventilation, the smell of orange peel, and the rudeness of the pit. England was having one of her periodical spasms of morality. There were many who trembled piously at the mere thought of being amused, who thought that no Christian was safe unless he was also dull. The theatre, like the ballroom, was the rendezvous for lost souls. The two hundred sects of Nonconformity were at least at one in their denunciations of the theatre, admittedly not without some justification. At the same time the Churches through their Young Men's and Young Women's Christian Associations were assiduously providing free and comfortable diversions as innocent alternatives to the theatre and the public-house, the two great moral enemies. This was one reason. Another was that during the summer season the theatre was to a great extent eclipsed by the musical predilections of one class and the rural excursions of another, while in the winter the increase in domestic comfort and home amusements kept the middle class by its fireside. The country gentry, who only came up to London from May till July, having for a long time known no music but the barking of the hounds, had become suddenly infected by a craze for the opera. And while the middle class stayed at home and read the latest novels from Mudie's Library, Society scrambled for boxes to hear the latest Italian prima donna.

An extravaganza entitled *Haymarket Spring Meeting*, by J. R. Planché, produced at the Haymarket Theatre in 1855, throws some light on the prevalent taste in entertainment. It begins with a song of which the refrain is:

This wonderful metropolis
Where everything is patronised except the Play.

It ends with a parade of runners for the Big Race. They are, in order of favouritism, Royal Italian (opera)—"That can't be English," comments somebody; "No," is the reply, "but he's the fashion"—then Foreign Opera (owned by Mr Meyerbeer), Mr Allcroft's Burlesque, Mr Webster's Fairy Tales, Mr Buckstone's Extravaganza, and Mr Kean's Romance. The field is completed by Mr Albert Smith's Mont Blanc and runners from the Panopticon, Polytechnic, and Panorama stables. As the betting on the stage proceeds some one remarks:

> Many managers are trembling now
> And may be posed, as it's both play and pay,
> To meet engagements upon settling day.

The legitimate theatre was, indeed, in a sorry plight. Some blame for its disfavour must undoubtedly be laid at the door of the profession. The art of acting had been allowed to deteriorate into mere declamation and stage business. A voice was almost everything. We read of James Anderson's "mournful, deeply impressive elocution," of John Ryder's "sonorous voice, deep, hollow, and tragic, varying in tone from that of an organ to that of a hunting horn," and of the "powerful organ" of the Hibernian Roscius, G. V. Brooke. Their orotundity seems to have been supplemented only by immense physical energy and stormy vehemence. Henry Morley, whose *Journal of a London Playgoer* (1851–66), is an invaluable record of the theatre of the period, writing in 1859 of *The Master Passion*, a blank-verse drama, says: "It was a grand thought to provide Mr Ryder so completely with a part to tear a cat in, and after setting him to rave through three acts make him burst in the last scene." And of G. V. Brooke's *Othello*, one of the last Shakespearean performances at Drury Lane before it became a circus, he writes: "It is a pity that he should prefer to act Shakespeare—for which he is as little qualified as the company engaged to support him—rather than a good, ranting, roaring melodrama, which he would play admirably. This would be infinitely better than making a melodrama out of *Othello*." One can understand why the discriminating playgoer began to shun the theatre.

Charles Dillon appears to have been the forerunner of a less violent school of acting. When he appeared in London in 1856 in *Belphegor*, a monstrous emotional drama in which he had made a provincial reputation for himself, it was his moderation that principally attracted attention. *The Athenæum* praised him especially for "speaking naturally, never noisily." "In these particulars," it said, "he presents new points and differs from nearly all English artists who have obtained reputation." *The Saturday Review* remarked that "greatly to his credit, he never gives way to the melodramatic temptations of a part abounding in sudden temptations of mood and passion."

Evidently actors found lungs and stamina more useful than brains. And clearly no satisfactory performance of anything but melodrama was possible under the system of "stars and sticks"—one or two famous players appearing as guest artists and supported by nonentities—when the former relied almost entirely on sound and fury, outdoing van Amburgh's lions, with which at one time they roared on alternate nights.

Between them these "unparalleled tragedians," as they were termed in E. T. Smith's hyperbolical billing, shouted Shakespeare off the stage. The two actor-managers who succeeded in bringing him back again in the fifties, Samuel Phelps and Charles Kean, belonged to a less rumbustious school of acting; in the latter's case this may have been fortuitously due to his being afflicted with a chronic catarrh. Phelps, on the other hand, deliberately cultivated a slowness of delivery, a measured pace of speech (which later hardened into mannerism) as he considered it necessary for the task of educating the ruffianly, slow-thinking audience of Sadler's

Wells to the enjoyment of dramatic poetry. This seemingly impossible task he accomplished, at first by leaving the stage and ejecting unruly members, and later by hushing them instead of overshouting them. Remembering Dickens's description of the Sadler's Wells public when Phelps began there, one must realize what an astonishing achievement it was to have popularized Shakespeare with that untutored rabble. The measure of it may be assessed by comparing Dickens's account with Henry Morley's description of the behaviour of the same audience, mostly composed of working men, which crowded the sixpenny gallery and shilling pit in 1853:

> There sit the working classes in a happy crowd, as orderly and reverent as if they were in church, and yet as unrestrained in their enjoyment as if listening to stories told them by their own firesides. *A Midsummer Night's Dream* abounds in the most delicate passages of Shakespeare's verse; the Sadler's Wells pit has a keen enjoyment of them, and the pit and the gallery were crowded to the furthest wall on Saturday night with a most earnest audience, among whom many a subdued hush arose, not during but just before the delivery of the most charming passages. If the crowd at Drury Lane is a gross discredit to public taste, the crowd at Sadler's Wells more than neutralize any ill opinion that may on that score be formed of playgoers. The Sadler's Wells gallery, indeed, appeared to be not wholly unconscious of the contrast, for when Bottom volunteered to roar high and roar low, a voice from the gallery desired to know if he could "roar like Brooke." Even the gallery at this theatre, however, resents an interruption and the unexpected sally was not well received.

During his eighteen years of management Phelps produced no less than thirty-four of Shakespeare's plays; all the First Folio plays with the exception of *Henry VI*, *Troilus and Cressida*, *Richard II*, and *Titus Andronicus*. Even *Pericles* was included in his repertoire! He was not perhaps a great actor, but he was certainly an intelligent one. As a producer his great merit was that he 'put over' Shakespeare at a time when this 'spelt ruin,' not as Edmund Kean and Macready had done by extracting from his plays all their inherent melodrama, but actually by stressing their poetry.

Phelps did not disdain the assistance of the scene-painter and the stage-machinist who were then beginning to acquire an unprecedented importance in the partnership of the theatre. His 'productions' were presented with a certain amount of splendour, as much possibly as his means would run to, though by no means with the lavishness of Charles Kean's Shakespeare 'revivals.' If there was any notable advance in the theatre of the 'fifties it was in the direction of scenic magnificence. Managers courted success by outdoing one another in 'effects.' In the Occasional Prologue to his *Alcestis* Talfourd satirized this growing tendency to pageantry.

> On gaudy pageants which elsewhere prevail
> We turn our backs as we unfold our tale.
> So the scene behind us is what it was before
> Wherein Greek meets Greek as in the days of yore.
> The spirited leaders of this o'erfast age
> Kicked o'er the traces of the slow old stage.
> Plays of the greatest and the least pretence
> Are mounted so regardless of expense
> That fifty nights is scarce a run accounted—
> Run! They should gallop, being so well mounted!
> In such fine feathers managers now show them,
> The authors of their being would not know them!

The shaft of Talfourd's wit is aimed particularly at Charles Kean, who took over the Princess's Theatre, in Oxford Street, in 1850, opening on Saturday, September 28, with *Twelfth Night*, preceded by a new farce and followed by a Ballet Divertissement. On the next Monday he presented

Hamlet similarly sandwiched. These were the start of a series of 'revivals,' whose merits were the subject of considerable controversy. Much of the poetry was cut, inevitably in a triple bill, but immense pains were taken to ensure an absolute accuracy in the matter of scenery, costumes, and detail. For example, in *Richard II* the John of Gaunt speeches were omitted, but the Lists at Coventry were reconstructed with the help of antiquarian advice, and horses borrowed from Astley's for the tourney. Also an "Historical Episode" was interpolated between Acts III and IV, in which Bolingbroke and Richard appeared riding through the streets of London amid the cheers and derision of the populace assembled in the street and in the windows of the houses. The *Illustrated Times* described the episode:

> Before the curtain rises the sound of a merry peal of joy-bells strikes the ear of the audience, not, be it minded, the mere tintinabulary orchestral substitute, but a real peal of bells, and when the scene is displayed to our view we find before us a street of old London, with the fronts of the houses adorned with tapestries and hangings, the balconies filled with gaily dressed citizens, and an excited mob filling the thoroughfare—awaiting the advent of Bolingbroke in the midst of a procession of delegates from various city companies and armed men of his own, bowing from his saddle-bow, and received with deafening plaudits by the crowd. After him follows Richard, who is assailed by hooting.

Kean said that he employed as many as 550 persons at the Princess's and spent in one season alone a sum little short of £50,000. The receipts for the theatre at one performance were considered large if they reached £200 and extraordinary if they reached £250.

The elaborate sketches of scenery, costumes and properties made for these revivals—now in the Victoria and Albert Museum and well worth studying—show the enormous care expended. They reveal that in the matter of stage production and the drilling of stage crowds the theatre of the 'fifties was by no means as benighted as is generally believed. Kean was, of course, attacked, as Irving and Beerbohm Tree were later attacked, for the spectacular nature of these revivals. *Punch*, which cherished a special antipathy for Kean, nicknamed him "the Great Upholsterer." His production of *Pizarro* in 1857 elicited from T. W. Robertson, then writing as "The Theatrical Lounger" in the *Illustrated Times* the comment: "*Pizarro* is one of the few plays which render us thankful to Mr Kean for the perfect manner in which he annihilates the original author."

On the other hand, his methods were defended on the grounds that "the days have passed when audiences could believe themselves transported from Italy to Athens by power of poetical enchantment without the aid of scenic appliances." Kean's earnest endeavour to combine entertainment with education was rewarded when he was made a Fellow of the Royal Society of Antiquarians, and the praise lavished upon him at a banquet given in his honour in July 1859 incited his inveterate critic *Punch* to make the rather feeble gibe:

BOARD OF HEALTH

Mr Charles Kean, we regret to say, has been very unwell since the night of his "Banquet," having on that occasion had to swallow a quantity of the rankest butter.

Opinions about the propriety of spectacular productions of Shakespeare have always been at variance, but in justice to Kean it must be remembered that at this time the craze for spectacle had invaded even opera. His *Richard II* in 1857, with its much-criticized interpolation of an "Historical Episode," was actually competing with a production of Verdi's opera *Il Trovatore*, played on horseback at Astley's.

It almost seems as if a successful theatrical production during this Hippodrama vogue had to be well-mounted in a double sense.

Despite these two largely disinterested endeavours in the cause of the declining drama—disinterested because neither Phelps nor Kean seems to have been primarily concerned with making money—it was still an ailing limb of the great body of literature. There were no dramatists of note. The writers of genius, who would have been playwrights in the Elizabethan era, were the novelists of the mid-nineteenth century. It had been evident for years that there was no longer a public for the conventional five-act, blank-verse drama. "Write me a drama," Macready had begged the young Robert Browning, "and save me having to go off to America." The drama was written, but reached only a fourth performance. Even the famous Bulwer Lytton's literary melodrama, *The Lady of Lyons*, failed to save England's greatest actor from his impending fate.

There was no temptation for the poet or the novelist to turn playwright. Playwriting was an unhonoured, unrewarding, and unlucrative profession. Even to the journeyman playwrights who catered to the public taste for burlesque, the most popular form of dramatic entertainment, the theatre brought little financial benefit. J. R. Planché author or part-author of fifty-seven extravaganzas and more than a hundred farces, melodramas, comedies, and opera libretti, was still in harness at the age of seventy-six and glad of a Civil List pension of £100. When Robert Brough, author of innumerable popular and often revived burlesques, died in 1860, although he had lived laborious days and was chargeable with no improvidence, he left his wife and children dependent on the proceeds of a benefit performance at which five London companies that had been indebted to his pen took part. Few playwrights supported themselves exclusively by their dramatic labours. They generally had some other occupation. The two most prolific and successful, the ubiquitous Dion Boucicault and Tom Taylor, were respectively an actor and a barrister. Few made any attempt at originality. Taylor, 'lifting' like his contemporaries quite unscrupulously from the French, had perhaps a happier knack than most of anglicizing his thefts and a dexterity in fitting any company of actors with a play suited to their particular talents and resources. Boucicault was plagiarism incarnate, borrowing his situations almost unconsciously from his vast knowledge of dramatic literature, ranging from Plautus to transpontine melodrama.

The drama, to the simple, unsophisticated audiences of the new industrial democracy, meant melodrama. They went to the theatre for the same reason as the farmers, cotton-pickers, and coalminers of Louisiana and West Virginia went to the show-boats of the Mississippi, as the modern cinema-goer visits the picture-house, or, for that matter, as the Elizabethan groundlings went to the Globe: because it was a place in which their secret dreams came true, a place where they could live a vicarious life of splendour, achievement, and of victory in love and triumph over wickedness, a place where they could shed tears unashamed and laugh uproariously, releasing long-pent-up emotions. They wanted, as such audiences have always done, the same things—love, passion, lust, and blood. They rejoiced in plays that were "all action, bounce, conventional stage chivalry, agony of the boards, pop, enter-at-the-nick-of-time, tableau and flummery, without a morsel of substantial thought or satisfying literature under it." The naïve spectator, uneducated to demand a rigorous causal logic in the theatre, untouched by modern cynicism, untrained in the appreciation of subtlety of characterization or acting, to whom the very word psychology was still unknown, shamelessly bedewed his whiskers with tears of genuine emotion at the grossest improbabilities and the sight of the most harrowing injustices unreasonably inflicted on his heroes and heroines. These plays were not literature; they were only a primitive kind of drama. But this was not a bad thing; art, like life, has sometimes to return to its childhood in order to be reborn.

The chief attraction of every melodrama of the period was its "sensation scene," a term introduced by Dion Boucicault from America. Its popularity justified Charles Kean's then-saluatry experiment in staging Shakespeare sensationally. These sensation scenes—for example, an exact reproduction of the Central Criminal Court with all the forms and furnishings of an Old Bailey trial (in *Janet Pride*, in 1855), or the representation of a blazing house with a real fire-engine at work extinguishing the flames (in *The Streets of London*, in 1864)—were achievements of stage realism never before attempted. Realism of a sort had, of course, been striven after much earlier—there is a record of "three vials of pig's blood and a sheep's gather" among the props required for a Jacobean tragedy—but never on so ambitious and elaborate a scale.

The artistry of such realism was questioned even then. In the stage version of Charles Reade's *It's Never too Late to Mend*, presented by Charles Kean's successor at the Princess's in 1865, "the horrors of prison life were exhibited in such minute detail that the delicately organized spectator was hit in the stomach rather than in the heart." This shocking realism was denounced by the first-night audience and in the Press. Notwithstanding—and how well this illustrates the unchanging morbid curiosity of the public—the management during the continuation of the run boasted in its publicity of the retention of the offending scenes, and daily published lists of the names of royal and noble patrons who had witnessed them!

Reading of these "dexterous feats of stage appointment for which our theatres in these days are remarkable," or studying the sketches for Charles Kean's Shakespearean revivals, one is inclined to wonder why the legend of Tom Robertson's "real door-handles" came to assume such an importance with the historians of the theatre. This craze for accurate reconstructions and imitations of reality was characteristic of the period when Robertson was still an impecunious prompter at the Olympic. It found its satisfaction variously at Madame Tussaud's and in the numerous dioramas and panopticons then in vogue. It was an extrovert age, and in two respects not unlike the Elizabethan. The coming of the railway and the steamship had made the world smaller, just as the voyages of the great Elizabethan mariners had done. There was a newly awakened interest in foreign countries and strange places. The diorama was the film travelogue of to-day. And just as the Renaissance had awakened a curiosity about the past in the Elizabethans, so the historians of the first half of the nineteenth century —Thomas Arnold, Grote, Thirlwall, Milman, Lingard, Hallam—had interpreted the past in a new way, not primarily for scholars, but for the general reading public. Macaulay's avowed aim, even at the risk of being reproached for having descended below the dignity of history, was "to produce something which shall for a few days supersede the latest fashionable novel on the tables of young ladies." It may be noted *en passant* that the latest fashionable novel came, as likely as not, from the pen of Miss Braddon or Wilkie Collins. The stage was not alone in catering for sensationalism.

Far more disgraceful, in the eyes of those who had the interests of the drama at heart, than the sensationalism of the public was its avidity for extravaganza and burlesque. There is an abundance of contemporary invective against these deplorable and vulgar travesties of Shakespeare, Grand Opera, the novels of Sir Walter Scott, classical mythology, and the fairy tales of the Victorian nursery. They were described as being:

> all leg and no brains, in which the male actor's highest ambition is to caper, slide, and stamp with the energy of a street-boy on a cellar-flap, the actress shows plenty of thigh, and the dialogue, running entirely on the sounds of words, hardly admits that they have any use at all as signs of thought.

The Pretty Druidess, a burlesque of the opera *Norma*, ends with this apology:

> So ends our play. I come to speak the tag
> With downcast eyes and faltering steps that lag.
> I'm cowed and conscious-stricken, for to-night
> We have, no doubt, contributed our mite
> To justify the topic of the age:
> The degradation of the English stage.
> More courage to my task I p'raps might bring,
> Were this a drama with real everything,
> Real cabs, real limelight too, in which to bask,
> Real turnpike-keepers, and real Grant and Gask.
> But no, the piece is commonplace, grotesque,
> A solemn folly, a proscribed burlesque!
> So for burlesque I plead. Forgive our rhymes,
> Forgive the jokes you've heard a thousand times;
> Forgive each break-down, cellar-flap, and clog;
> Our low-bred songs, our slangy dialogue;
> And—above all—oh, eye with double barrel,
> Forgive the scantiness of our apparel.

It is obvious why the historian of the drama should ignore burlesque; but the chronicler of the stage cannot dismiss a form which enjoyed continuous popularity for over sixty years. And to preserve our perspective we must ask the question: Were the best of them less witty and less intelligent than the revues of Noel Coward or Alan Melville? Were the worst of them more stupid and more vulgar than some present-day road-shows? The authors of many of these burlesques of the 'fifties and the 'sixties were men of wit, contributors to and even editors of *Punch* and its then companion journal, *Fun*. *The Pretty Druidess* was the work of W. S. Gilbert. If Sir Alan Herbert had been born in 1830 would not he, like Gilbert, have served his apprenticeship as a writer of burlesque?

Let us therefore accord burlesque the dignity of a dramatic species, for, rising from the subordinate and occasional position which it shared in its beginnings with pantomime, of Christmas or Easter piece, it came to hold equality, at least as regards the permanence of its attractions, with the other branches of the drama. Burlesque began under a various nomenclature in which there was doubtless a nice distinction that now requires very sharp discerning: Fairy Extravaganza, Classical Burlesque, New and Original Burlesque Pantomime, Operatic Extravaganza, etc. In the hands of Planché, who dominated the earliest phase of the burlesque, the stories on which they were based were treated with a certain respect; he boasted that he had never distorted them. His treatment was always in good taste. The cleverness of the burlesque writer consisted in making the sublime (in classical burlesque) easy and familiar rather than ridiculous or grotesque, and the marvellous (in Fairy Tale burlesque) matter-of-fact, and in giving a topical seasoning to Shakespearean parody. Planché was as content to write for the reward of a smile as of a belly-laugh—a rare virtue in a comic writer. His talent lay in the direction of revue, a term which, if he did not actually invent it, he gave to his *Seven Champions of Christendom*, a political allegory produced in 1849, a premature experiment in a new *genre* which has never found much favour on the

English stage. He had an ovbious affinity with Herbert Farjeon, whose version of *Cinderella* is in the Planché tradition. Curiously, he had ambitions to "lay the foundations of an Aristophanic drama," to raise the extravaganza to a high level of satiric comedy. It was, he admitted, "a hazardous experiment, but one worth making for the sake of art and the interests of the British stage"; but he misjudged his own powers and the nimblemindedness of his audiences. Satire has never proved congenial to the British theatre crowd.

The Planché burlesque was a witty and also rather a pretty thing, for his favourite subject, the Fairy Tale, called for prettiness. The second school of burlesque, which we may call the Brough school (for Robert Brough was its chief and best exponent), retained only so much of the plot of the original story as secured for the piece interest as a story, while each incident, large or small, was gently metamorphosed by a flash of wit, a humorous twist of thought or phrase, reason, or rhyme, or a lunge of satire. This school saw the burlesque as one long unflagging *jeu d'esprit*, and gave the actor the chance of elaborating a character that should be as consistent with itself and as true to nature, in spite of the fantastic and grotesque bedizening, as any character in the more realistic branches of the drama. In a burlesque of *The Merchant of Venice*, for instance, and again in *The Yellow Dwarf*, that pathetic little comedian, Fred Robson, was able to give performances which revealed the potentialities of a really great tragedian. When he was acting at the Olympic, at a time when the aristocracy eschewed the theatre, a long line of coroneted carriages crowded to the doors.

With the third and last school of the late 'sixties and 'seventies the conservation of plot was to a great extent discarded, and the spectator, losing interest in the production as a whole, was reduced to the necessity of extracting fun out of each incident. And as the difficulty of the process increased, the author had to spice each incident accordingly in order to put it over, as, for example, by the introduction of characters that had no intrinsic value in the plot and by providing them with songs and eccentric dances. So burlesque degenerated into a medium for bringing together a number of eccentricities of wit and clowning, more or less clever in themselves, but otherwise incongruous. In a word, as time went on, the burlesque lost sight of its chief purposes, parody and allusion to the political and social topics of the day, and lapsed into buffoonery. Charming nonsense and natural merriment became vulgar tomfoolery and the mechanical humour of more and more outrageous punning. The signs had begun early. Already in 1861 Planché protests: "If we are to be plunged into jungles of jingles and sloughs of slang, all I demand is not to be accused of having set the example."

Punning—for the pun was always the backbone of burlesque—seems to have been almost a vice of the age. Even Parliament was affected. *Punch* once translated the abbreviation M.P. as "miserable punster." And, as puns perforce became staler, burlesque punned itself to death. The pun was put into cold storage, to be resuscitated fifty years later by the radio comedian. Punning at its best, however, is a lost art. We may think less ill of it as a form of wit if we examine this passage from William Brough's historical burlesque *The Field of the Cloth of Gold*. King Francis, lost in the forest, has this soliloquy:

> These fine old trees my view on all sides border;
> They're Foresters of the Most Ancient Order.
> Still, for their king thus trapping there's no reason;
> And so, *high trees*, I charge you with *high treason*.
> My royalty at least there's no mistaking;

I've walked till every bone tells me *I'm a king*.
I'll lie down 'neath these boughs, for I protest,
Walking this *forest long*, I *long for rest*.
Francis, full length extended 'neath these branches,
Will be what's called *Extension of the Franchis*.

Harley Granville-Barker once commented on this passage
in a paper written for the Royal Society of literature.

There is much art in the cumulative effect of this. 'Ancient
Order of Foresters' is, of course, not a pun at all. *High trees
—high treason* is a straightforward one, the pun direct; *till
every bone tells me I'm a king* is the 'pun implied' for variety;
forest long—long for rest is the 'pun reversed.' But it is all a
preparation for the sheer impudence of *Extension of the Franchis*
which should strike us 'twixt wind and water, and the skilled
actor will see that his audience does not laugh till then. For
the tasting of the joke's full flavour the play's date must be
remembered: 1868.

What was the nature of the audiences who patronized
burlesque? It goes without saying that they were mostly
male. Henry Morley characterizes them as "Mr Dapperwit
in the stalls, Lord Froth in the boxes, and Pompey Doodle
in the gallery." Wilkie Collins in *My Miscellanies* speaks
of "the fast young farmer from the country and the convivial lawyer's clerk." That they were not without some
pretensions to fashion is shown by the fact that in *William
Tell* (Lyceum, 1857) "Mr Shore, playing one of the peasants,
carried an ivory-handled cane, fifty facsimiles at least of
which were to be seen in the pit." That they were quick-
witted in the best days of burlesque is also clear. The better
extravanganzas were written by intellectuals for intellectuals. They were frequented by the Bohemians who con-
gregated at the Garrick, the Arundel, the Savage, and the
Fielding, and met at Tom Hood's Friday supper parties;
men of the world whom the world bored, officers who

found the military clubs too solemn, and the night-birds of the law, the Press, and literature. The vulgarities for which Gilbert apologized only crept in when the burlesque was past its prime. The burlesques of Planché, Talfourd, the two Broughs, and Robert Reece relied on their wit, the genuine comic value of their ideas, their neatness of parody, and the freshness of the punning.

The true burlesque form was a one-hour entertainment without interval, sometimes elaborated into two sets for more scenic display. It came on in the middle or at the end of a triple bill, timed for the convenience of late-comers, primed with a good dinner. The later tendency to drag it out to undue length, to over-decorate and over- (or under-) dress it, hastened its decline, no less than its increasing vulgarity. As audiences became more mixed a stronger flavour was required for coarser palates. Alfred Austin succinctly described these later audiences as "the half-drunk leaning over the half-dressed." As burlesque deteriorated more and more into a leg-and-slapstick show, the moral tone of the burlesque theatres sank so low that they lost their patronage.

It was only later that burlesque acting became a specialized branch of the profession. In the 'fifties and 'sixties an actor was expected to appear in anything from domestic drama to farce, from *King Lear* to pantomime. In his first London engagement in 1865 John Hare appeared in a petticoat-rôle as Zerlina, a simple peasant girl, in H. J. Byron's burlesque of *Don Giovanni* and in farce. He also created the part of Lord Ptarmigan in Tom Robertson's *Society*. In 1866 Charles Wyndham, fresh from service as an army surgeon with the Northerners in the American Civil War, supported Miss Pattie Oliver in F. C. Burnand's burlesque of Douglas Jerrold's *Black Eyed Susan* at the Royalty. In 1868 Robert Reece's *The Stranger; Stranger than Ever*—a burlesque of a much-parodied play by Kotzebue—was produced under the direction of the author and a Mr H. Irving. The actors and actresses who made their names at the Strand, the Royalty, and the Olympic in the 'fifties and the 'sixties were to be the accomplished comedians and comediennes of the next two decades. Among them were Marie Wilton, Lottie Venne, Mrs John Wood, Edward Terry, J. L. Toole, and Lionel Brough. Only later, when burlesque acting included singing and dancing, did it become a special study and provide a training school for the musical comedy which succeeded it.

In reflecting on the low state of the drama at this time— "There are no plays," said some one, "only plays on words; no dramatists, only playwrights pilfering without compunction from the French"—it must be taken into consideration that the eighteen-fifties, like the nineteen-thirties, were a period of political tension. Victorian England had not yet settled down after the industrial unrest of the Hungry 'Forties. It still felt the reverberations of the Continental revolutions of 1848. These years were also war years: they were disturbed by the Crimea and the Indian Mutiny. The prevailing taste was the taste of anxious times. "The insane desire for amusement at any price," remarks *The Spectator* in 1857, "is imagined to be the reaction of the parsimony and quiet living during the War Years"; and adds "What would be the result if we could now get rid of the Income Tax?"

The chief reason, however, was that there was not a sufficiency of educated theatre-goers. Society had to be won back to the habit of theatre-going. The ban of fashion had to be lifted, religious prejudice overcome. The two new sober-minded classes, the prosperous merchant and the superior artisan who astonished the French painter, Delacroix, by dressing like a gentleman—the stalls and the pit of the theatre of the 'eighties and the 'nineties—had still to be attracted to the theatre. The railroads brought to London a large floating population, but it was made up of sightseers rather than seekers of intellectual recreation. Yet the theatre was by no means stagnant. This was a period of progress, both technical and histrionic; of advance in realistic production and in the art of the scene-painter. The 'sensation' drama challenged the producer to attempt scenes never before attempted on the stage. The designs for Kean's revivals and for Lord Byron's *Sardanapalus* are amazingly advanced. They pointed the way for Sir Henry Irving and Sir Herbert Beerbohm Tree, and suggest that in the handling of stage-crowds, no less than in scholarly authenticity, Kean broke almost virgin ground. There was also an advance in acting. The actor in the new and smaller theatres began to unlearn the declamatory, stentorian, and gesticulatory methods, the 'magnoperation' necessitated by the enormous size of the old patent theatres, where the performer was out of ear- and eye-shot to the greater part of the house. He began to acquire subtlety. The triple bill at almost every theatre and the constant change of rôle taught him versatility. The peculiar technique required for burlesque gave him experience in that most valuable asset of the comedian's equipment, the art of perfect timing.

At any given moment in the history of the theatre it will be found that either the playwright, the actor, or the producer is in the ascendant. In the 'fifties the playwright was a licensed thief, a plagiarist journeyman. It was said at the time by those who remembered Edmund Kean, Kemble, and Macready that the race of good actors was extinct, that there were not half a dozen equal to those parts in which the language rose above the commonplace or where there was a demand for anything not to be found in the usual assortment of conventional emotions. There was, however, an unprecedented opportunity for the stage-designer and the machinist, who had tremendous fun with wires and pulleys, slides and trap-doors, making fairies and angels float and ghosts appear and disappear, and adapting to stage use the Optical Illusions exhibited by Professor Pepper at the Polytechnic. But apart from such merely accessory tricks they were trying, as it were, to discover a new dimension: to give to the stage scene perspective, as the new toy, the stereoscope, did for the photograph. It was their heyday rather than that of the producer, who did not exist in our sense of the word, indeed the word was never used. It was largely owing to their "novel feats of stage appointment" that the theatre was able to attract a new, if untutored, public sufficiently numerous to put it financially on its feet. And that was a step forward.

II

THE PEEP OF DAWN

The Eighteen-sixties

ON October 27, 1860, Henry Morley noted in his journal: "Next week the accusation against the public that it does not support the stage will be met by the fact, unprecedented, I believe, for many years, that in the winter season all the theatres in London from Her Majesty's to the Soho are open together." The play-going public was increasing rapidly. London was growing, and the crowd of strangers daily passing through it was so large that it might easily take a year to make room in one of the bigger theatres (such as Her Majesty's, which could seat three thousand persons by the houseful) for all those desirous of seeing a play reputed to be good. On an average the public going in daily detachments to the theatre numbered at least 15,000. All classes were gradually becoming theatre-conscious, with the exception of a still reluctant section of the educated class, and, of course, a section, every year diminishing, of persons who retained, in a religious abhorrence of theatrical performances, the tradition of a time when there was honest reason why the theatre should be in bad repute.

New theatres were springing up and old ones being reconstructed. In a decade and a half the number of playhouses in London was nearly doubled. One theatre after another began to lose its old aspect of discomfort before the curtain. The chief cause of discomfort was the tendency of

37

certain managements to crowd their seats together. In their desire to reap the quick fruits of every success they filled even the few narrow gangways with extra chairs and standing room. Packed like sardines in an ill-ventilated theatre, the audience stifled in the heat from the new gas lighting. Catch your customer, truss him, stew him four hours in a hot closet—that was the prevailing recipe.

The following theatre note is culled from *Punch*, December 1, 1860:

> As Mr Punch had no idea of missing the French play or of being suffocated while at it, he took a little gherkin in his pocket, but the fearful heat so operated on the vegetable, in a forcing point of view, that it grew into a cucumber big enough to supply supper to his party of five.

The manners of the audience had notably improved except for the ineradicable habit of sucking oranges during the performance. But the quality of the plays that filled the theatres showed little improvement in the public taste. When Frank Matthews, himself a good actor and supported by a capable company, became lessee of the St James's Theatre with the laudable ambition "to produce the best new plays he could get of a creditable sort," the curtain rose one evening to an audience of five in the stalls, seven in the dress circle and thirty in the pit. Abandoning his policy, he put on a double bill, consisting of *Lady Audley's Secret*, a melodrama so tightly packed with such thrills as bigamy, murder, arson, and the madness of the heroine that "the pudding was all plums," followed by a burlesque of Dion Boucicault's *The Trial of Effie Deans*, an Old Bailey melodrama concocted out of Scott's *The Heart of Midlothian* —and played to crowded houses. Melodrama was so popular that in 1864 a training school had to be created for cast-replacements for *The Ticket-of-leave Man*, when, after a run of 406 performances in London, road-travelling com-

panies were formed for the first time to take this unprecedented success into the provinces with their own scenery.
Sensational melodrama was the trump card to draw the
town. Even the long day of the Hippodrama had ended.
In 1863 Astley's was taken over by Dion Boucicault and
transformed into the Theatre Royal, Westminster, for the
opening of *Effie Deans*, a venture which, according to the
promises of the persuasive author-manager who introduced
the term "commercial management" into theatrical parlance, was to show his trustful backers how thirty thousand
million or billion—or whatever dazzling sum it was—
represented the natural annual profits of a right system of
management.

Spectacle was still a good second card. Even the burlesques were being mounted lavishly. Planché complained
that he was being "painted out of existence." The spectacular was a gilt-edged insurance. It saved the worst play
from downright failure; allied with wit or well-proved
situations it guaranteed success.

As at all times when the low condition of the drama had
been deplored, the blame was thrown on the vitiation of
public taste. "If," Colley Cibber remarked at another ebb-
tide period of the drama, "the public by whom they must
live had spirit enough to discountenance and declare against
all the trash and fopperies they have been so frequently
fond of, both the actors and the authors, to the best of their
powers, must naturally have served their daily table with
sound and wholesome diet." A public without epicurean
experience can, however, hardly be expected to show itself
fastidious. But the point was not really that the public was
pleased with trash, but that what was offered to them in the
name of drama was earnest and respectable, but very second-
rate work. And this, though it had entertained their
fathers, bored the new public. And there was one indication

that Phelps's patient training of an audience capable of appreciating well-spoken poetry and the more delicate shades of expression proper to the actor's art had not been fruitless labour. In 1863 he appeared at Drury Lane in Lord Byron's *Manfred*, and despite the poem's lack of effective dramatic action of the ordinary sort it was received enthusiastically by packed houses. It was, perhaps, the first sign that there was a demand for serious drama, and in those days serious drama meant poetic drama. But as yet there were no authors to supply it. The blank verse dramatists were merely inferior disciples of Bulwer Lytton and Sheridan Knowles. The writers of comedy were even more insignificant. They attempted no reflection of the manners of contemporary society. They went on copying *ad nauseam* their old masters, Sheridan and Goldsmith, or their new masters, Scribe and d'Ennery. They limited their characterization to a few conventional stage types, suited to the speciality of the leading comedians, who varied their performance only by exaggerating their idiosyncrasies with each new play. The most successful comedy of the early 'sixties, Tom Taylor's *Our American Cousin*, owed its success solely to the buffoonery superimposed by Sothern upon the thin framework of the part of Lord Dundreary.

The revival of comedy came about by a "concatenation of fortuitous circumstances." Miss Marie Wilton, the darling of the Swanborough burlesque company at the Strand—whom Charles Dickens, writing to John Forster in 1859, declared "the cleverest girl I have ever seen on the stage in my time, and the most singularly original"—tired of playing principal boys, and unable to persuade managers that she had any assets other than a roguish eye and a pair of nimble legs, made up her mind to launch out on her own. Not only Dickens, but also Planché, Mark Lemon, and Shirley Brooks had drawn attention to her talent, but the

managers, like the public, could only see a graceful little
lady dancing jigs. She had, however, a devoted following
among the Bohemian intelligentsia and a good friend in
H. J. Byron, then virtually resident playwright—or rather
play-upon-words-wright—of the Strand. The two entered
into a partnership; Miss Wilton brought to it £1000 borrowed from her brother-in-law, and Byron his reputation,
puns, and promise of new material. With this they acquired
the lease of a bankrupt and almost derelict theatre in the
noisy and squalid district off Tottenham Court Road, then
beginning to collect a shabby and shady foreign population.
The theatre which rejoiced in the impressive title of "The
Queen's" was known locally and more appropriately as
"The Dusthole." It was renamed the "Prince of Wales's,"
cleaned and restored, fitted with "four commodious rows
of stalls, consisting of fifty-four in number, all spring-
stuffed and cushioned, and covered with blue leather and
white-enamelled studs, the box seats, entirely new, similarly
stuffed and covered; and the whole circle, brilliantly illumin-
ated, lined with rosebud chintz."

On the historic date, October 21, 1865, while the queue
was already forming outside this blue-and-white *bom-
bonnière*, the new manageress was still hammering in the
last nail with her own hand. The opening bill showed no
promise of making theatrical history. Its *pièce de résistance*
was a "new and original operatic burlesque" from the pen
of H. J. Byron, preceded and followed by a one-act farce.
Miss Wilton's friends and admirers loyally supported her
and there were many carriages waiting in the mud of
Tottenham Street. The occasion was reported in the
Illustrated London News as "the most stirring event of the
season."

But Marie Wilton had not yet shown her hand. To be
more accurate, she had not yet a hand to show. Her opening

programme soon exhausted its attractiveness, and when she turned to Byron for fresh material, very fortunately as it proved, that indefatigable provider was otherwise committed and generously recommended his friend, T. W. Robertson. Robertson was the son of an actor—in his own words, "nursed in rose-pink and cradled in properties." The theatre was in his blood as it was in Byron's. The two were friends of long standing. They had acted and starved together; they had even unsuccessfully collaborated as dramatic authors. While Byron, five years the younger, had already achieved success, Robertson was still ekeing out a precarious livelihood by prompting, comic journalism, dramatic reportage, and making adaptations of French plays. His only successes had been as a talker at Tom Hood's supper parties and with *David Garrick*, an adaptation of the French play *Sullivan* for Edward Sothern. His only original play, *Society*, had been submitted to Buckstone at the Haymarket who had returned it with "Rubbish!" scrawled across the manuscript and the assertion that it would not reach a fourth performance. The faithful Byron had, however, persuaded a provincial manager to take a chance with it, and it had gone down fairly well in Liverpool. *Faute de mieux* Miss Wilton put *Society* into the bill on November 11, 1865, as *hors d'œuvre* to the usual Byronic operatic burlesque, and therewith not only established the success of her little theatre, but started a new era in English comedy. *Society* ran for 150 performances. It was followed almost at once by *Ours*, which lasted through the theatrical season of 1866–7, and then in turn by *Caste* (1867–68), by *School* which surpassed its predecessors in popularity, being played nearly four hundred times, and finally by *M.P.* in 1871, the year of Robertson's death.

The first night of *Society* made something of a sensation. Was it solely the emergence of a new playwright which set the drawing-rooms of Belgravia, Bayswater, and Kensington gushing and sent the Forsytes and the Jolyons in their broughams into that uncharted and disreputable quarter? For this was the significance of its success for the future of the English stage. Certainly the new plutocracy with its rigid standards of good taste and notions of gentility had been waiting for a play to which they could safely take their wives and daughters, and Mr Robertson's "refinement" was especially emphasized in the favourable notices of his play. "The combination of dialogue so brilliant, repartee so pungent and sparkling, expressions so refined, characters so full of repose, yet so distinctly drawn and stories so pure, yet so enthralling in their interest"—these in contemporary opinion were the outstanding qualities of Tom Robertson's genteel, middle-class comedies. But the players must share the honours. A writer, describing the first night of *Society* makes this revealing exclamation: "Think what it was to see a bright, cheery, pleasant young fellow playing the lover to a pretty girl at the time when stage lovers were nearly all sixty and dressed like waiters at a penny ice-shop!" This bright, cheery, pleasant, and well-dressed young fellow was a new-comer to the London stage, a Mr Bancroft, who, it appeared, was actually a gentleman, not only in bearing, but by birth and breeding. Twenty-four, tall and slender, with an air of aloof distinction and well-bred nonchalance, Bancroft was soon wildly romanced about. Everybody's cousin had been at Eton or Harrow with him; everybody else's brother had served in the same cavalry regiment. Young ladies turned their heads demurely to stare at him in Bond Street.

In his own person Mr Bancroft was an encouragement to gentlemen to enter the profession. But he was no Society amateur, like the Hon. Lewis Wingfield, who had lately outraged Society by publicly appearing in burlesque and making a disgusting exhibition of himself in petticoats. In four and a half years as a provincial actor he had played 446 rôles. He had learnt his business thoroughly and the hard way. He was responsible also for the intelligent realism introduced into the scenery of the Prince of Wales's productions. To him must be given the credit for the famous handles with doorknobs.

There was also another new star discovered in this brilliant little firmament—John Hare. Hare had an extraordinary gift of mimicry and facial expression, particularly, even when young, for the portrayal of the eccentricities of age. His art might have missed fire in a bigger house, but this little bandbox of a theatre was exactly suited to its subtlety. He appeared in *Society* as Lord Ptarmigan, a part only very broadly sketched by Robertson, which became what Hare made of it. He consolidated his reputation as Prince Petrovsky in *Ours*, as Sam Gerridge in *Caste*, and as Beau Farintosh in *School*. These parts were in a real sense 'creations' of the actor—as distinct from the specialized type characterizations of the comedy actors of the old school. Such was the brilliance of the cast at the Prince of Wales's that the appearance in small parts of a later famous actor, William Terriss, passed unremarked.

And what of Marie Wilton, the ex-principal boy who had forsworn burlesque? After *Society*, Robertson's plays were tailored for the company with skill, each character fitted with the utmost nicety to the man or woman who was to play in it. He very wisely furnished Miss Wilton with *gamin* parts and allowed her full reign for her particular talents. In *Ours* she took part in a game of bowls, mimicked the affectations of the swells of '65, played at being a soldier, basted a leg of mutton from a watering-can, and made a roly-poly pudding adapting military implements to culinary uses for the purpose. In *Caste*, as Polly Eccles, she sang, danced, boxed people's ears, played the piano, pretended to blow a trumpet, put on a forage cap, and imitated a squadron of cavalry. In *School* she climbed a wall. And these burlesque interpolations added enormously to the fun of Robertson's comedies. In fact their charm depended largely on his full utilization of his material and his personal inspiration. W. S. Gilbert, who admitted that he had learnt the art from Robertson, said:

> He invented stage-management. To-day it is called production. It was an unknown art before his time. Formerly, in a conversation scene, for instance, you simply brought down two or three chairs from the flat and placed them in a row in the middle of the stage; the people sat down and talked, and when the conversation was ended the chairs were replaced. Robertson showed how to give life and variety and nature to the scene by breaking it up with all sorts of little incidents and delicate by-play. I have been at many rehearsals and learnt a great deal from them.

The Prince of Wales's was the first theatre deliberately aiming to attract a fashionable audience. And it was the happy coincidence of all these factors: the bright and comfortable intimacy of the theatre itself, the good manners, tastefulness, and careful detail of the production, the freshness and gaiety of the team acting, the romantic glamour attaching to the leading man (presently enhanced by the marriage of Marie Wilton to her handsome *protégé*), the impression of back-stage gentility—all new things—in a word the atmosphere of elegance and refinement, that made the erstwhile Dustbin the Mecca of a family threate-going public. It was just such a public the theatre needed to attract, if it was ever to replace the taste for the absurd and the extravagant by a taste for sentimental comedy.

Robertson's home-brewed comedies were just their cup of tea. This colloquialism is here singularly apt, for the new form was soon dubbed "Teacup and Saucer Comedy," a name which suggests the wholesome and mildly stimulating beverage of polite intercourse and genteel persiflage. It was something entirely novel. These stories of the joys and sorrows of ordinary unromantic people, stories of youth and age, of love, parting, and reunion, of modest acts of chivalry and self-sacrifice, the whole stippled with a thousand humorous and pathetic touches, yet narrated in language devoid of ornament and set in surroundings of the most commonplace description—however naïve and 'wishy-washy' they may seem when read to-day—had a peculiar freshness and truth to the audiences of their time, accustomed to the flashy theatricality and stilted verbosity of the class of play then known as "domestic drama." This was the cup that cheered and made no effort to inebriate. It did not strive after a sensationalism like the imported melodramas; its humour was of a different order from the elementary boisterousness of bowdlerized French farce. Robertson's achievement was in bringing to the stage his natural talent as a conversationalist, his gift of repartee, his observations of the world he was familiar with—soldiers, theatrical folk, artistic and literary Bohemians—drawing from life instead of copying conventional stage models. This "Realism," more than the realism of locks and door-knobs, was new, for we know the exact date of the birth of this kind of scenic realism: January 3, 1831, when Madame Vestris at the Olympic abolished the wings and hung real curtains in place of painted drapes, laid real carpets on the boards and furnished the scene with period furniture. No; Robertson's innovation was not in any strict fidelity in the mounting which was probably anyhow Bancroft's doing, but in the fact, to quote a contemporary observer, "that the scene-painter, the carpenter and the costumier no longer usurp the place of the author and the actor." The success was a two-sided one. Robertson provided the talented company at the Prince of Wales's with truthful parts and they interpreted them with truthfulness. Both the playwright and the actors were pioneers. Robertson initiated a new school of realistic drama, and the new style of realistic acting introduced a lasting change. The two were complementary. The one would not have succeeded without the other. But, as Tom Taylor wrote to the young manageress on the day after a fresh triumph, the author and the theatre, the actors and the rôles, all seemed made for one another.

The "Teacup and Saucer Drama" drew into the theatre a new *clientèle* from the drawing-rooms of Society, a fashionable and more fastidious public, whose cultivation was of great importance to the future of the theatre. Not least important was the readiness and ability of his new public to pay higher prices for their seats. When in 1880 the Bancrofts had outgrown the Prince of Wales's and took over the Haymarket, they were able to abolish the pit (already backed by Mr Webster in 1852), which had occupied the best part of the house at a minimum charge, and to raise the price of the stalls successively to six and seven shillings, and eventually to ten and sixpence. This revolutionary step not only led to greater comfort for the patrons of the theatre, but also made possible a raise in actors' salaries and ultimately in authors' fees as well. Mrs Stirling, who created the part of the Marquise de St Maur in *Caste* at the Prince of Wales's, received a salary seven times as large at the Haymarket when the play was revived there. This new trend, made possible by the attraction of a new class of audience, caused Douglas Jerrold to remark to the veteran comedian, Charles Matthews: "I do not despair of seeing you yet with a good cotton umbrella under your arm carrying your savings to the bank."

The Bancrofts unwittingly performed another service to the English stage. When they went on a provincial tour during their first holiday from the Prince of Wales's they happened to be playing in Liverpool at the time of the autumn assizes there. The young London barristers who followed the circuit, most of whom had long numbered themselves among the staunchest supporters of Marie Wilton, at once gathered round their idol. On one of the convivial evenings spent together an impromptu mock trial was staged, presided over by the ex-queen of burlesque in judicial wig and robes. Among these young barristers was one named William Schwenk Gilbert. Gilbert, who was treading the higher walk of the legal profession and was still waiting for the profession to embrace him, supplemented an illusory income by working on the staff of *Fun*, of which his friend H. J. Byron was editor. No doubt he entered whole-heartedly into the spirit of this frolic, if he did not indeed inspire it; and later when, like the penniless barrister of the Judge's song, he "tired of third-class journeys and dinners of bread and water," he made good use of the memory of that evening in a one-act dramatic cantata which he called *Trial by Jury*. It was set to music by Arthur Sullivan. Though it is too much to suppose that this occasion first turned his thoughts to writing for the stage, it was his acquaintance with Tom Robertson that was responsible for his first venture as a playwright. In 1868 Miss Herbert, then lessee of the St James's Theatre, invited Robertson to provide her with a Christmas entertainment, and he, being unable to comply, recommended Gilbert, just as Byron in like case had suggested him to Marie Wilton. The result was a burlesque of Donizetti's opera *L'Elisir d'Amore*, called *Dulcamara, or the Little Duck and the Big Quack*, completed in ten days. It was followed by several more operatic burlesques, *Robert the Devil*, *The Merry*

Zingara, or the Tipsy Gipsy and the Pipsy Wipsy (on *The Bohemian Girl*) etc. and a pantomime, *Harlequin Cock Robin and Jenny Wren*. Gilbert was content for the time being to follow the conventional pattern of the burlesque, with its songs written to popular tunes and traditional airs, its jingling rhymes, and atrocious puns.

Adina in *Robert the Devil* sings to the air of "The Sugar-shop":

> If you intend to stay with us, before you've been a day with us,
> You'll learn the proper way with us, of saying what you say to us.
> Each speech should have a pun in it, with very foolish fun in it,
> And if you can't bring one in it—you'd better stay away.

Gilbert could pun with the best or the worst of them. His burlesques are hardly distinguishable from those of his contemporaries, though here and there the authentic, if immature, Gilbert is discernible, especially his fondness for the dactyllic rhyme, as in these lines from *Dulcamara*:

> Oh, animosity and villainous verbosity,
> Perpetual precocity and fabulous ferocity,
> And venomous velocity and every other -ocity,
> In planning an atrocity or compassing a crime!

There are the puns and foolish fun. The conventions of burlesque forced him to use all the vulgar expedients on which the theatres, famous for this kind of entertainment, had so long relied, but he was fully alive to their vulgarity, and, remembering his objections to writing words to Sullivan's music, one may imagine how he chafed under the handicap of having to fit his lyrics to well-known tunes. "The Sugar-shop"—whatever that was—seems to have been unusually suitable for the Gilbertian rhythm.

Writing under the pen-name of Thumbnail Sketcher in *London Characters*, Gilbert let fly at the indiscriminate applause cheaply evoked:

A claptrap sentiment, a burlesque breakdown, a music-hall parody, a comic man coming down the chimney, an indelicate joke, a black eye, a red nose, a pair of trousers with a patch behind, a live baby, a real cab, a smash of crockery, a pun in a 'comedy,' an allusion, however clumsy, to any topic of the day, a piece of costermonger's slang, or any strongly marked tailoring eccentricity, is quite sure of a rapturous reception whenever it is presented to an audience.

These were the things he was determined to kill, but some fifteen years were still to elapse before he dealt burlesque its first death-blow with the Savoy operas. Gilbert had yet to experiment with various dramatic forms before he lit upon the one best suited to his genius. Had his gifts been different or his attempts in that line been more successful he might well have become merely a disciple of the "Teacup and Saucer school." His first straight prose play, *Sweethearts* (1874), shows the intention, but it also revealed Gilbert's inability to depict love or reproduce its language. He lacked Robertson's natural touch in dialogue; his was too stiff and formal, too carefully contrived; and his temperamental cynicism, for all that he was a sentimentalist at heart, made sentimental comedy impossible for him. But in *Engaged* (1877) there was something absolutely original. It was coldly received. Critics disapprovingly called it a "cruel farce," though one, more perspicacious than the rest, described it as "one of the most riotously humorous, whimsically incongruous, utterly comical burlesques it has been my lot to see and read." Gilbert could never quite escape from burlesque. Even his greatest success, *Pygmalion and Galatea* (1871), was said to "halt inconsistently between the romantic and burlesque methods." Moy Thomas, however, dramatic critic of *The Graphic*, declared it "a very bold as well as a very successful experiment upon the tastes of audiences." The success of this fantasy was due in no small measure to the appearance of Madge Robertson, the young sister of the dramatist, then in the flower of her twenty-second year, together with Kendal, whose wife she was soon to be, as Pygmalion; but it was not an unequivocal success. The public which looked for sentiment found the satire too astringent. The Victorians were not averse to fantasy; they loved Alice and Edward Lear and Gilbert's own *Bab Ballads*. But, as G. K. Chesterton pertinently pointed out: "Alice in Wonderland is not Alice in Utopia; she is not in an ideal country which challenges and satirizes her own country. Lear's landscapes and travels are really in the other end of Nowhere: not in Somewhere disguised as Somewhere Else." It needed Sullivan's music and the immense pains taken by Gilbert to get the details of costume, scenery, and movement authentically right to half-conceal the fact that *The Mikado* was a satire on the English. It is a comic fact that it was actually forbidden in 1907 because it was a satire on Japan.

Gilbert was not a great and serious dramatist although he may have had the idea at the back of his mind that this was the case. All the same his contribution to the drama was more valuable than may appear. In the opinion of Sir Arthur Quiller-Couch:

> Before he turned to libretto, Gilbert in his lighter plays, unrewarded by applause, did perhaps as much as his friend Robertson to break up by solvent the turgid tradition of mid-Victorian drama and expose its theatricalities. It is usual to ascribe the revolution to Robertson. But Robertson, although he shows a glimmering light towards such reality as exists in 'realism,' did not—being himself a sentimentalist—probe the real disease of sentimentality. It was Gilbert who probed it and applied the corrosive; and the corrosive proved too strong at first for public taste; perhaps because it confined itself to destroying the fatty tissue without any promise of healing.

III

A MILDER MORNING

The Eighteen-seventies

ROBERTSON was now recognized as the pre-eminent dramatist of his generation. Sixteen years previously he had been glad to assign all rights in an unplayed drama for the sum of £3 cash. He was now receiving the standard author's fee of £3 a night from the Prince of Wales's. In 1870 Buckstone, the veteran manager of the Haymarket Theatre, belatedly attempted to repair his error of judgment over *Society* by putting on a play by the author of that phenomenally successful piece. He offered Robertson the unprecedented sum of £10 a performance for a new comedy. Once again he backed the wrong horse. *Home* was an adaptation and a failure.

On the very night that *School* had its three hundredth consecutive performance at the Prince of Wales, his "sensational drama," *The Nightingale*, was booed at the Adelphi because "the audience's apathy with the early action of the play gave way to amazement at the absurdity of the situations and indignation at the actions of certain characters." Robertson, having changed the public taste, now curiously tried to cater for the taste he had been foremost in destroying. He was then a dying man. Mrs Bancroft, who accompanied the ailing playwright on the opening night recalls his standing pathetically, livid with fury, shaking his fist at the hissing audience and muttering: "I shall never forgive them for this." He died the following year at the age of forty-four.

It is impossible to overlook the fact that without the Prince of Wales's ensemble his plays (with the exception of *David Garrick*, which was an adaptation from the French) were failures. He had little dramatic invention. He was a skilled miniaturist who could not paint on a broad canvas. His sorcery left him when he ceased to handle cups and saucers. The tiny Prince of Wales's, half theatre and half drawing-room, was ideally suited to his essentially modern method, that of bringing clearly into focus within a definitely bounded field of vision a chosen phase of life. It would be surprising that so small a thing as was the Robertsonian comedy should have been so important a landmark in the history of the theatre if it had not been the first use of what Henry Arthur Jones aptly termed "the eavesdropping convention." The way for intimate comedy had been prepared by the better lighting of the stage. In the vast, dim-lit barns of the old theatres the play had been mainly auditory. David Garrick's introduction of footlights—or floats, as they were first called—made the players more visible, but it was gas-lighting that made the play really visual. The change was immensely important to the actor. The new "intensive" art, which was one name given to it, achieved its effect, like the Dutch school of painting, by the magnification of detail. For this it was necessary that the manipulation of cups and saucers should be visible to the back row of the gallery. Intensive plays require little theatres.

So, as the vogue for Robertsonian comedy naturally encouraged its imitators, little theatres came into existence, like the Charing Cross Theatre, "a little glove-box," opened in 1869. And for a while the fashion lingered for the naïve portrayal of the actions, dress, and manners of ordinary life, for plays twinkling with sentiment and humour, and devoid of all violent emotion. With the production, also in 1870, of a "dainty, domestic comedy" by a young and unknown playwright it seemed that the mantle of Tom Robertson had fallen on the shoulders of James Albery. *Two Roses*, a chocolate-box title typical of the sentimental trend, ran for fifteen months and 'held the boards' throughout the 'seventies and the 'eighties. In *Two Roses* an unknown actor, Henry Irving, attracted some attention in the comedy part of Digby Grant, but less than several other members of the cast, notably "handsome" Harry Montague, who was hailed as "bringing the hot-house aroma of Mayfair over the footlights"—an indication of the impression created by the "Teacup and Saucer school" of acting. In this case the praise, for praise it was meant to be, is as amusing as it is instructive of the trend of acting-fashion. "A confounded amateur, laddie!" was for long the verdict of the older Thespian on Bancroft. But Bancroft, if never a great actor, was by no means an amateur. Montague was just that. He was probably the first to step straight from the boards of an amateur stage into a leading West End rôle, and it can only have been his amateurishness that suggested the Mayfair hothouse aroma, for he was originally a city clerk. His subsequent career was, as might be expected, undistinguished, and he has no interest for us except to point the lesson that personal charm and unstudied nonchalance are not in themselves a sufficient equipment for the professional stage; the danger of the Robertsonian school was that it encouraged the belief that they might be. Forty years later, when the same danger threatened the stage, Harley Granville Barker wrote:

> Acting seems so easy and, like all other art, ought in its accomplishment to seem easy. In its inception, moreover, to the unsophisticated, happily unselfconscious young person dwelling in the false paradise of artistic innocence it *is* so easy

that to plunge into the practice of it without having fully faced, not so much its difficulties as its possibilities, is inevitably to run the risk of developing one's innocence not into knowledge, but into an experienced and hardened ignorance.

Irving knew this instinctively. When he first made up his mind to become an actor he had the offer of an engagement from Phelps. He refused it because he realized the necessity of serving the usual novitiate in the provinces. And then, after three years of study and provincial drudgery, in which he played 128 different parts from Shakespeare to pantomime, he threw up his first six-line part in London because he preferred a return to that salutary mill to the stultifying routine of repeating the same lines evening after evening.

To go back to James Albery: *Two Roses* was followed the next year by *Apple Blossoms*, and this by *Two Thorns* and *Forgiven*. But each fresh addition of hot water to the teapot only resulted in a more insipid concoction. Perhaps these comedies proved, as the critic of *The Athenæum* reflected, that "of all forms of dramatic untruth that of ultra-realism" —how funny that sounds in this connexion to-day!—"is in its effects the most completely disillusionizing. Like the waxwork figure nodding a welcome at the entrance of a waxwork exhibition, the motions that at first gave the idea of life take away by the continuance all possibility of belief in it." Perhaps they proved William Archer's dictum that "the Robertsonian school of playwriting illustrates no point in dramatic art except the possibility of keeping an audience of Britons amused with cleverly flippant and feebly sentimental small-talk," a possibility which no one who knows the theatre is likely to dispute, but which is best exploited in troublous times—among which Albery's period, the years of the Franco-Prussian War, may be included. Stirring times have never been the inspiration of stirring drama in our century. Time and again the English theatre-going public has taken refuge from the meditation of grave events in the contemplation of domestic tittle-tattle. But, anyhow, Albery proved himself to be only a one-act playwright. He had neither the concentration nor the pertinacity needful for the mastery of his craft. His brief career as an original dramatist closed with the failure of *Jacks and Jills* when he, too, "stood up, white with rage, before the curtain, denouncing the 'organized opposition' which had damned his play." Robertson had vowed that he would never forgive the audience that hissed *The Nightingale*. The public never forgave Albery his exhibition of ill-temper. He is a striking example of a dramatist spoilt by initial success. The playboy playwright doubtless knew his inherent weakness and that play-writing is, like acting, hard, unremitting work, when he composed his own epitaph in fun:

> He revelled 'neath the moon,
> He slept beneath the sun,
> He lived a life of going to do,
> And died with nothing done.

Archer, who had a curiously high opinion of Albery's ability, admitted that "his fancy was too luxuriant to be kept within bounds by his rather deficient sense of dramatic propriety." It is a little difficult to understand the furore created by *Two Roses* except as a swing of the pendulum from the blood-on-the-bread-knife drama to the kettle-on-the hob drama. Probably it just fitted the quieter taste of the time. It coincided with the vogue for Trollope's novels, the beginning of the period when, as R. L. Stevenson said, "English people are apt, I know not why, to look somewhat down on incident, and reserve their admiration for the clink of teaspoons and the accent of the curate." Still more difficult is it to comprehend Archer's declaration that "beside Albery at his best Robertson at his best is as apollinaris to champagne."

It is, perhaps, interesting to sample the dialogue of this period. To the modern ear Albery's seems a constant straining after epigram. Here are three examples of his euphuism:

Do you know that Cupid's wings have so often been wetted with the tears of betrayed maidens that he has caught rheumatism in his shoulders and has no longer strength to draw his bow?

Flowers are made by angels and smell of their fingers.

A naval officer offers to wager "a silk cable and spin it myself though I have to live on mulberry leaves for a month."

These are fair samples of the champagne. Luxuriant fancy, if you like, but strangely out of keeping with ultra-realism! Let us compare them with a draught of apollinaris, a soliloquy spoken by the journalist, Tom Stylus, in *Society*:

Love is an awful swindler, always drawing upon Hope, who never honours his drafts; a sort of whining beggar continually moved on by the maternal police; but 'tis a weakness to which the wisest of us are subject, a kind of manly measles which flesh is heir to, particularly when the flesh is heir to nothing else; even I have felt the divine damnation—I mean emanation. But the lady united herself to another, which was a good thing for me, and anything but a misfortune for her. Ah! happy days of youth. Oh! flowering fields of Running-ton-cum-Wapshot.

It is curious that at this time, when the drama had ceased to be considered a literary art, to find, even in comedy, this straining after literary dialogue. Nothing dates so quickly as stage dialogue. Certainly to readers of Disraeli's novels it sounded less precious than it does to-day. It shows how difficult it was for the stage writer to rid himself of the idea that he must be literary. Literary pretensions were the curse of the serious dramatist. But one can see what an advance there must have been that anyone could think of it as ultra-realism. It is assuredly more lively than the flatulence of Bulwer Lytton, whose *Money* was still being continually revived and from which we cull this specimen:

> My friends—we must confess it—amidst the humours and follies, the vanities, deceits, and vices that play their parts in the great Comedy of Life—it is our own fault if we do not find such natures, though rare and few, as redeem the rest, brightening the shadows that are flung from the form and body of the TIME with glimpses of the everlasting holiness of truth and love.

This taste for epigram and artificially turned phrases was no bad thing. In one direction comedy was tending towards the representation of actuality, in another towards Oscar Wilde's desideratum, "art divorced from life." The epigram and the literary veneer helped to bring drama back into the literary fold and culminated in the plays of Wilde himself.

It might be thought that with the success of the unknown James Albery's maiden comedy the door had at last been opened to the original English playwright. For several decades the word 'original' in its true meaning had been absent from the playwright's dictionary, just as the word 'impossible' was absent from Napoleon's. H. J. Byron's first venture in the field his friend Robertson had pioneered, *Cyril's Success* (Globe, 1868), was printed with a dedicatory preface amusingly concluding with the words: "I beg to remind anyone who may care to recollect the fact that *Cyril's Success* is original and a comedy . . . in five acts! There!" But despite the triumphs of original comedy in the Prince of Wales's and at the Vaudeville, and the further fillip given to native domestic comedy when Mrs John Wood, "that diverting low comedian in petticoats," fol-

lowed Marie Wilton's example, turned her back on burlesque and became the lessee of the St James's Theatre (also
in 1870), originality was very severely handicapped. The
fact was that the playwright could not afford to write
'on spec.' He was called upon by contract to supply an
established company with dramatic material. He had to
take the measure of its different members and to fit them
out as nearly as he could from the readjusted fripperies of
which his closet was full. He had to drag into his play
unnecessary characters simply because there were at hand
competent expositors of a mechanical formula to which
comedians adhered and to which the author had servilely
to readjust his parts. The would-be original playwright
thus found himself required merely as an author-tailor. His
plays became inevitably rearrangements of familiar bits of
material. "The author," said W. S. Gilbert, "must set
aside anything in the shape of parental pride in his work,
and must be prepared to see it cut up and hacked about by
the stage-manager without caring to expostulate."

Furthermore, in the early 'seventies the theatre had begun
to be an interesting financial speculation. Many mushroom
managements sprang up, helped by the ease of opening a
theatre and the readiness of tradesmen to give credit to
theatre managers. These newcomers, being in the theatre
from mercenary motives, had no interest in discovering
new dramatists. They looked, as is always the case with
their kind, to past successes or to foreign importations. It
was only in desperation that one of them put on an original
play. Gilbert described this kind of manager in a rather
bitter sketch in which he supposes the author of an unsuccessful play on trial before a jury of the audience. He is
charged with "having written and caused to be produced
an original stage play which has not come up to the expec-
tations of the audience." The most amusing part of it is

the cross-examination of the manager by the author. The manager says:

> I did not read your play before accepting it, because I do not profess to be a judge of a play in manuscript. I accepted it because a French play on which I had counted proved a failure. I had nothing ready to put in its place. I was at my wits' end. I have been there before. I soon get there. I have had no special training for the position of manager. I am not aware that any special training is requisite. It is a very easy profession to master. If you make a success, you pocket the profits; if you fail, you close your theatre abruptly, and a benefit performance is organized on your behalf. Then you begin again.

There was also another motive for entering into theatrical management. Many noblemen took this way of securing the right to enter the theatre at pleasure instead of waiting at the stage door, and all they asked of an author was that he should furnish some lady to whom four lines had been hitherto refused with a reach-me-down piece in which she could play the leading rôle. And when written it would be thrust on to the stage in a crude state, and virtually rehearsed before the public, from which it received the corrections that ought to have been supplied by the management. These young ladies were advanced from burlesque and were drawn, if we may believe Gilbert again, exclusively from the tribe of "principal girls." He describes the "principal boy" as

> a bright, intelligent girl who sings a little, dances a little, and can give a pun with proper point. Her manner is perhaps a trifle slangy and her costume just a trifle showy, but her character is irreproachable. She is a good-humoured, hard-working, half-educated, lively girl who gives trouble to no one. The Principal Girl is simply a showy fool, intensely self-satisfied, extremely impertinent, and utterly incompetent.

[How one would like to have seen Gilbert dealing with one of these!] However, as a set-off to these drawbacks she must be an admirable domestic economist, for she contrives to drive her brougham and live *en princesse* in a showy little cottage *ornée* on £3 a week. These young ladies are the curse of the theatre. They are the people who bring the actress's profession into contempt; who are quoted by virtuous but unwary outsiders as fair specimens of the ladies who people the stage.

The position of the would-be original playwright in the 'seventies was similar to that of the British song-writer in the nineteen-twenties and -thirties when music-publishers' shelves were stocked with bought American tunes. Theatrical managers' drawers were stuffed with bought French plays. Having actually invested money in M. Chose's latest farce or M. Machin's melodrama, which was 'pulling in' the boulevards, all they wanted of an author was a workable adaptation. Adaptation was far more lucrative than composition. The adaptor of Erckmann-Chatrian's *Le Juif Polonais*, which when produced as *The Bells*, by H. L. Bateman, at the Lyceum in 1871, made Irving famous overnight, was a down-at-heel solicitor who lived on this solitary achievement and Irving's bounty ever after. By the Copyright Act of 1852 a foreign author retained the copyright in his work for five years, but this applied only to translation and not to adaptation. This word was by no means clearly defined, and an adaptor had only to transpose two scenes and suppress a character of the original to avoid paying copyright dues. In 1875, however, the five-year copyright was extended to cover adaptation as well as translation with the result that there was less importation of foreign plays. This helped the English playwright to get an original play considered.

Until this came about the sought-after playwright or

author-tailor was far too busy executing commissions to be able to think seriously of himself as a dramatist. For instance, Tom Taylor, who scored his first success in collaboration with Charles Reade in 1852 with a "merry and right-minded little comedy," *Masks and Faces*, had since been writing industriously for the stage, dramatizing French novels, anglicizing French farces and melodramas, and even composing hippodramas; he had done everything, in fact, for twenty years except write an original play. And he was a man of culture, Professor of English Literature at University College, barrister-at-law, Secretary of the Board of Health, and sometime editor of *Punch*. Now suddenly he decided that it was time to write for posterity, and with that strange obliquity of vision which characterized the aspiring serious dramatist of the time, turned to the composition of historical dramas. Original tragedies in blank verse . . . and, of course, in five acts! There! *Twixt Axe and Crown* and *Joan of Arc*, written for an actress generally alluded to as "the beautiful" Mrs Rousby, soon passed into oblivion. They won for the veteran author no literary palms. Some critical indignation, however, was aroused by the crude realism of the nightly roasting of Mrs Rousby at the stake as the Maid of Orleans. A.W. Pinero, who saw both these plays, wrote afterwards: "I never could make out whether I was listening to prose which sounded like verse or verse which sounded like prose."

Only among authors did the idea subsist that there was still life in blank-verse drama. When in 1869 Barry Sullivan, the last great tragedian, "consulted his own reputation and the honour of his country by providing at the Holborn Theatre a legitimate arena for classical productions," it was soon evident that classical productions were out of fashion. Even Shakespeare was in eclipse. Sullivan was compelled the following year to rely on *Behind the Curtain*, of which the plot was "a farrago of crimes committed by preposterous characters acting on inadequate motives, the action scarcely intelligible, the moral tone objectionable, and the representation of the life it purposes to depict unnatural and untrue." "The drama of the present," writes Hawk's Eye in *The Stage in* 1871, "is almost entirely supported by the educated middle classes who do not like tragedy." And yet the ambitious literary playwright continued to be hypnotized by the blank-verse, five-act tragedy, believing that Shakespeare had chosen the five-act form and that blank verse was a kind of stove-pipe hat of respectability. Even the Poet Laureate, Alfred Tennyson, who now at the age of sixty-five devoted himself to writing for the stage, made the mistake of going to school to Shakespeare instead of trusting his own native dramatic instinct.

The wrong-headedness of these disciples of the Bulwer Lytton and Sheridan Knowles tradition lay partly in their wearisome pretension of fine writing and their aloofness to the theatre—many affected incomprehensibly to write for the study rather than for the stage—and partly in their inability to recognize that the blank-verse drama was an obsolete form simply because the effects which the poet had formerly had to create with poetry could now be created by the scenic artist. As the play became visual as well as auditory owing to the better lighting and the smaller size of the theatres, the allowance permissible to narrative was reduced to a minimum. With the picture-frame stage the tide ran in the direction of spectacular realism. The taste of the time, under Gallic influence, was for quick and constant action. Dumas, Eugène Sue, and (in England) Harrison Ainsworth, had stepped up the pace of dramatic history. The change was visible even in melodrama. Edward Falconer's once immensely popular *Peep o' Day*, which on its first production in the 'fifties ran for a year, when revived in 1870, failed because "modern audiences seek incident alone and are as a rule intolerant of anything that delays or suspends the action."

And yet how many persisted with their soporific verse, their "windy suspirations of forced breath," synthetic exercises in a defunct tradition! It is sufficient to name H. C. Merivale, Westland Marston, LL.D., and the minor poetess, Isabella Harwood, who under the pseudonym of Ross Neil wrote fourteen verse-tragedies, of which only one was ever performed. Irving declared in 1880 that he was overwhelmed with five-act dramas, "many by authors who proudly claimed that they made a point of never going near a theatre." The indefatigability of the closet dramatist is all the more incomprehensible because at that time there was no reading public for plays, and, in fact, except in French's sixpenny edition of acted plays, no plays were published, and there was not in London, as there was in Paris, an Odéon or a Théatre de Cluny where the rejected might appeal to audiences eager for unappreciated merit. Even W. S. Gilbert could not resist the epidemic. His blank verse play *Gretchen*, a version of the Faust legend with Mephistopheles left out, flopped egregiously. "How did it end?" a listener kept asking when Gilbert was explaining his treatment of the story at his club. "In a fortnight, sir," snapped the author, annoyed by the interruption.

Still, when doctored by the actor-manager, who was now about to oust the theatrical entrepreneur and who considered his responsibilities to include a virtual part-authorship, verse-drama was not entirely dead. The most sought-after poetaster-playwright was W. G. Wills, a cousin of Oscar Wilde, who had become in effect the resident dramaturge of the Lyceum in that he was the first playwright to draw a yearly salary from a theatre. Though his natural leanings were towards literature rather than towards the stage, he was one of the busiest play-manufacturers of his time. He had some theatre-sense and was helped by Irving's knowledge of the mechanism of the stage. He provided Irving with one of his greatest successes in *Charles I*, in which he wisely dispensed with the comic underplot hitherto thought necessary as 'relief' by the poet-dramatist. The play no doubt owed its success to Irving's moving portrayal of the Martyr King. As Philip of Spain the actor again secured a modified success for the Poet Laureate's *Queen Mary*. That he had a decisive hand in the final construction of both plays is known. Wills, who was incapable of handling a situation effectively once he had found it, though he was endowed with considerable inventiveness, wanted to end his play with a tableau of the execution of the King outside Whitehall Palace. Irving, possibly mindful of the outcry against the crude realism of Mrs Rousby's roasting, was obdurate in his objection to this. The problem was solved by Bateman, still the lessee of the Lyceum and technically Irving's manager, who, when the three were discussing this knotty point one night at supper, suddenly snapped his fingers and exclaimed: "I've got it. The parting of William and Susan in *Black Eyed Susan*." And so the last act, the parting of Charles I and his weeping queen, was modelled upon the sailor's farewell to his sweetheart in Douglas Jerrold's old and long popular melodrama.

Tennyson, diffident in his awareness that he had no practical experience of the theatre, wrote with the intention that his plays should be edited by the actor; in *Queen Mary* twenty-seven of the *dramatis personæ* were liquidated by Irving, a great deal of meditative poetry was jettisoned, and the ending made theatrically effective. Irving's biographer insists that the excisions were made by the poet himself under Irving's guidance, but tales were told of the aged poet contending for dear life for his ewe lambs as the actor serenely and ruthlessly insisted on further slaughter.

The most important theatrical event of the 'seventies was the return of Shakespeare with Irving's appearance as Hamlet in 1874. It was a revolutionary performance, immediately recognized as marking the final abandonment of the old traditions of acting and of the declamatory convention. "If the style Mr Irving adopts of giving Shakespeare's soliloquies," wrote E. R. Russell, "is that of the future, we in England are as far ahead of French art as we were in the days when Talma learnt in England the lessons he transmitted to France and on which the French school is founded." With *Hamlet* Irving initiated a new manner of Shakespearian representation. Its rightness was the subject of much debate; its modernity and unconventionality were provocative. It revived an interest in Shakespeare which had lapsed after Charles Kean retired a sadder and a poorer man, and Phelps relinquished his apostolic work at Sadler's Wells. *Hamlet* ran for two hundred nights.

But the occasion was something more than the arrival of a great actor who had waited long enough for recognition. His greatness had been recognized two years before when he saved Bateman from financial disaster by his performance in *The Bells*. His biographers may, however, be pardoned for dramatizing the first night of *Hamlet* as the triumphant scaling of the last rung of the long ladder to acknowledged fame. It certainly made him the Fashionable Tragedian. The same licence may be claimed to dramatize it as a decisive victory for the Theatre over the prejudices that had so long prevailed against it, the cue for the restoration of the stage to the favour of the upper classes. It also gave the profession a leader, which it had not had since Macready's death in 1856. It established the Lyceum in the position forfeited by Drury Lane as London's premier theatre.

Although this *Hamlet* was mounted economically as compared with its later revival and Irving's subsequent Shakespearian productions it was nevertheless a departure from the old-fashioned, cheese-paring methods that were the rule at this time at every theatre except the little Prince of Wales's; it was the starting-point of a new, liberal, artistic, dignified way of presentation in keeping with the luxurious tendencies of the age. It brought back to the theatre the world of fashion which had disdained it for over a quarter of a century. Within a few years the glittering *premières* at the Lyceum were to be the outstanding feature of the London season, culminating in the première of *Faust* in 1886 when there were "frantic efforts, grovellings, implorings, etc." to obtain a seat. A peer was actually seen in the gallery and was more than content with his seat. The Royal Family were in their box, and the Prince, then in mourning, watched the play from behind the scenes. Even the Puritanical abstentionists, firm in their abhorrence of this form of entertainment, and persistent in their prejudice even against the theatre as a building—thousands of them witnessed plays when given at the Crystal Palace—relaxed their taboo to exclude the Lyceum. Pantomime was for some curious reason not regarded as the theatre, and presently during the Gilbert and Sullivan régime the Savoy was looked upon as 'safe.'

Reading the contemporary praises of the Bancroft-Robertson productions, one cannot help being struck by the reiteration of the word 'refinement.' The recurrent qualification in contemporary appraisals of Irving's productions and of the acting in them after he took over the management from Bateman in 1878 is 'distinguished.' Irving gave *tone* to the theatre. He dignified the social position of the actor. He also dignified the managerial attitude towards the public. He treated his patrons, not, as other managers had been accustomed to do, as a tradesman casual customers to be exploited by charging extras for booking fees and programmes (the practice at every theatre except the Haymarket, St James's, and Gaiety), but as a liberal host his guests, catering for their pleasure and comfort with every aid that taste and money could supply.

Not the least service Irving did to the theatre was to introduce a strict discipline at the Lyceum. Gilbert did the same at the Opera Comique and the Savoy. The old happy-go-lucky, slap-dash methods of production, unpunctuality at rehearsals, and unbusinesslike conduct of the theatre were replaced by a disciplining to a standard of all-round efficiency hitherto unthought of. It was copied by other actor-managers and made possible the phenomenal advance of the theatre towards the end of the century.

The junior members of Mr Irving's company (among whom were Forbes Robertson, George Alexander, and Martin Harvey) learnt this discipline at "St Lyceum"—as his theatre was soon mockingly canonized by the Gaiety girls across the road. They basked in the reflected distinction of their chief and in their private lives enjoyed something of the limelight denied them on the stage. Their financial status was not similarly enhanced. The rise in actors' salaries begins with the Bancrofts' tenancy of the Haymarket in 1880. 'Supers' were still fifteen bob a dozen per performance. Very few members of the Lyceum company drew a double-figure weekly salary. Irving himself began with Bateman at £15 a week, raised to £35 after the success of *The Bells*. But the actor began to be accepted into society as in turn the stage began to draw recruits from it. At the banquet given on the stage of the Lyceum in celebration of the hundredth night of *The Merchant of Venice*, at which all fashionable London was present, Lord Houghton, proposing the health of the new "gentlemanly"

Shylock, rather tactlessly commented on the general improvement in the social status of the profession which had been, he declared, so marked that "families of condition are ready to allow their children to go on the stage." Three years later the *Gentleman's Magazine* gave expression to some concern regarding the possible effects both on art and on society "now that the actor is established in the boudoir and exhibited in society." In 1885 a quaint little booklet appeared, entitled *The Actor's Vade Mecum*, by F.B. of the Theatre Royal, Clapham, "Being Advice to Persons who have adopted the Stage as a Profession how to Behave in Polite Society and Elsewhere."

Under this influence paterfamilias began to revise his long-cherished opinion of the actor as an impecunious wastrel and of the actress as a brazen hussy; he actually put his sons and daughters into the once-despised profession.

The genteel stage aspirant at this time found his or her initial opportunity in 'walking on' in those scenes of melodrama which were supposed to represent polite society. They were known to the Profession as "Adelphi guests." These superior "supers" of both sexes, who for a shilling a night—he in white cotton gloves and she in a shabby gauze dinner dress—moved extensively in stage upper-crust assemblies between the Strand and St James's Street, now disappeared and were replaced by whole groups of young people eager for an 'appearance': the young gentlemen from the public schools and universities, the young ladies from country parsonages and gentle life. The term 'extra ladies and gentlemen' supplanted the old term 'super.' Fashionable teachers of elocution and the art of acting flourished.

Two types of advertisement began to appear sporadically in the newspapers: the one inserted by the stage-struck seeking a back entrance introduction to the theatre, the other by spiders hopeful of devouring these innocent flies. Here are two specimens:

> A YOUNG LADY, of good voice, figure, and stage appearance, wishes to meet with a lady or gentleman who can introduce her on the stage. No managers need apply. Address Alice, Pitman's Library, 140 Gower Street, W.C.

This appeared in *The Times* in February 1878. The curious proviso forbidding the direct approach of managers suggests that Alice was living in Wonderland.

The second is culled from the *Daily Telegraph*, 1874:

> THEATRES—TWELVE LADIES and GENTLEMEN WANTED, to support a star actor. Totally inexperienced persons may write.—Apply by letter only to Tragedian.

It was not long before Clement Scott was driven to complain in the *Fortnightly Review* that "the old-fashioned, conscientious actor, full of stage traditions, devoted to his profession, and caring nothing for social recognition, is thrust to the wall by sprigs of the aristocracy and society school-girls, who neither possess natural aptitude nor trouble to acquire it," and that in consequence modern acting showed a falling off in earnestness, reality, and power. Supply was following demand. In the old days all that was needed in order to appear as a stage gentleman was to be properly dressed, to know how to wear a sword and carry a cane, make a bow to a lady, and swear a round oath to a lackey. A much higher standard of civilized behaviour was now required. Frederick Wedmore, writing on "The Theatrical Revival" in the *Nineteenth Century Review* in 1883, regarded it as a hopeful sign that secondary parts were being played more and more by players of breeding and gifts.

The modern young actor, then making his appearance in the theatre, brought with him not the hothouse aroma but the cool aplomb of Mayfair. Irving told the story of his engagement of one such for the part of Horatio before seeing him act. After reading over his part in the first scene, Irving said: "Now you try it. I will take the Ghost." And the young man "apostrophized me in the most cool, familiar drawing-room, conventional style possible to imagine. I was aghast. There was nothing to be done but engage another performer." The phrase "modern young actor" is Irving's own. That does not mean, however, that Irving was an old-school die-hard, like Jack Ryder, for example, then teaching elocution and dramatic art in the Adelphi. In the 1879 production of *The Merchant of Venice* at the Lyceum exception was taken to the "conversational method of elocution" adopted by the subordinate characters, who were found to "rattle through the poetical lines of the Bard in a sort of hurried chatter to the general loss of dignity." Similarly, admirers of the obsolescent gesticulatory and declamatory school of acting regretted the "painful dissonance" of Irving's own delivery. There was a startling modernity also in his refined and gentlemanly Shylock, compared with the crouching, dilapidated Fagin of tradition; a Shylock who, instead of flourishing his knife like a butcher in the Trial Scene, handled it more like a surgeon with a scalpel.

The more cultured audiences newly being attracted to the theatre would not have stood for the obstreperous methods and exaggerated emphasis of Ryder's day when the chief organ of apprehension was the ear rather than the eye. But now *migravit ab aure volupta somnis ad incertos oculos et gaudia vana* (all pleasure has shifted from the ear to the illusive eyesight and unsubstantial delights), from which it would appear that a similar change occurred in the Rome of Horace. Irving was fortunate in that one of his most effective gifts was his ability to present character without exertion or 'acting' in the old meaning of the word. His greatest power lay in his gift for facial expression, a play of features exhibiting the processes of thought, his face anticipating every change and rendering the following speeches mere illustration. "Acting," he once said, "is like billiards. You get over the table into position with your cue before you make a stroke, and in acting you want to prepare the minds of your audience for what you say before you say it." His merits as an actor were hotly disputed. The same extremes of violence as characterized the later controversy over Ibsen led his admirers to declare that he had exhausted the possibilities of acting; his detractors to assert that he could not act at all. They said he mumbled; they said he could neither talk nor walk. His legs became a famous subject of caricature. In this connexion an astute remark of Henry Labouchère's seems worth quotation:

> An actor must, in order to win popularity, have mannerisms, and the more peculiar they are, the greater will be his popularity. No one can for a moment suppose that Mr Irving could not speak distinctly and progress about the stage after the manner of human beings, and stand still without balancing to and fro like a bear in a cage, if he pleased. Yet, had he done all this he would—notwithstanding that there is a touch of real genius about his acting sometimes—never have made the mark he has. He is, indeed, to the stage what Lord Beaconsfield was to politics. . . . Were Mr Irving at present to abate his peculiarities, his fervent worshippers would complain that their idol was sinking into the commonplace.

Irving was able in an astonishing way to identify himself with the soul and spirit of his creations, projecting the passionate remorse of Mathias, the purged suffering of King Charles, the senile devilry of Louis XI. He could even suggest a different physique, height, and figure. As Napoleon he trotted rapidly around with quick and nimble feet, hingeing his gestures from the elbows and wrists; as Charles his stride was long, slow, and majestic, his gestures hinged from the shoulder. His Dante walked leaning forward and held his left shoulder a little higher than the right. Each character looked absolutely different from another and from himself. And yet he was always Irving. If this was to some extent deliberate, as Labouchère suggested, it shows how well he realized also the secondary technique of the actor's art: his personal relation to the public, the winning of its sympathy for the actor himself behind the parts he plays, which, when won, inspires the illusion of an intimate acquaintanceship.

Irving brought the actor back into a place of paramount importance in the theatre. In considering the charge that he did nothing for the drama, that, as Shaw said, he was only interested in the exploitation of his own personality, it must be remembered that at the time—and this may be largely true of any period—people went to the theatre more for the sake of the acting than of the play. "The revival of interest in the actor's art," notes the *Gentleman's Magazine* in 1883, "is perhaps the most remarkable of social phenomena." It was stimulated by the performances of Irving and also by those of several illustrious foreign visitors to London: the great Italian actor, Salvini, the American nonpariel, Edwin Booth, and the Comédie Francaise with Mounet-Sully and Sarah Bernhardt, and by the publication in 1883 of Walter Pollock's translation of Diderot's famous *Paradox sur le Comédien*. It culminated in a public argument between Irving and Coquelin, which was academically rounded off in William Archer's *Masks and Faces*, published in 1888. It spread to the universities. Edinburgh, whose university not many years before had censured Professor Blackie for lecturing on the drama and introducing students to Aristophanes, invited Irving to lecture at the Philosophical

Institute in 1881. And in 1886 the popular Master of Balliol, Dr Jowett, then Vice-Chancellor, after the rejection by two votes of his proposal that the university should confer an honorary degree on Irving, invited him to deliver an address at commencement, and directly the lecture was over "surprised every one by getting up and supplementing it with a defence of the drama." One of the results of Jowett's championship was the foundation of the O.U.D.S., following a performance of Æschylus's *Agamemnon* with the undergraduate Frank Benson as Clytemnestra, in 1882.

One notes that Irving was chosen for these honours as representative of the drama, not the theatre. Yet once he answered the reproach that he failed to aid the new English drama with the curt reply: "Damn the English drama!" His own view of the function of the stage he gave in an address to the Perry Bar Institute, Birmingham, in 1878:

> To the common, indifferent man, immersed as a rule in the business and socialities of daily life, it brings visions of glory and adventure, of emotion, of broad human interest. To all it uncurtains a world, not that in which they live and yet not other than it, a world in which interest is heightened and yet the conditions of truth are observed, in which the capabilities of men and women are seen developed without losing their consistency to nature, and developed with a curious and wholesome fidelity to simple and universal instincts of clear right and wrong.

Now these conditions were amply satisfied by melodrama, with its emphasis on adventure and emotion, and the simplicity of its moral psychology. The modern, who has lost faith in the comfortable providence that rules in melodrama and does not believe that we live in a world in which things fall out fitly, scoffs at it. He is alienated by its irrational optimism just as he is estranged by the thoughtful optimism of Meredith and Browning. The modern, who has been brought up on psychological novels and thinks in terms of Freud, finds the self-sacrificing heroes of melodrama as absurd as its sinister villains. But the Victorian accepted them. He liked to believe in poetic justice and to have stage-characters labelled sheep and goats. Ten years later Henry Arthur Jones wrote:

> In 1880 one would have said that there was not a sufficiently large section of the theatre-going public interested in dramatic art as distinguished from mere entertainment; sufficiently adept in that most interesting of all studies, the study of humanity, to make it worth while for a playwright to risk his reputation by attempting to give a representation of life instead of the stale devices of the theatre that they are so used to and love so well.

Irving arrived at a transition period in the theatre. Matthew Arnold in his famous article in the *Nineteenth Century Review* in August, 1879 wrote: "We are at the beginning of a period and have to deal with the facts and symptoms of a new period on which we are now entering; and prominent among these facts and symptoms is the irresistibility of the theatre." But note that this article by a leading man of letters was not a plea for an intellectual theatre, but for the theatre of *l'homme sensuel moyen*, the average sensual man, "with the fireworks of fine emotions, grand passions and denouement lighting it up when necessary." Irving completed the *visual* education of the theatregoer, who was only later to be taught to bring his mind into the theatre as well as his emotions and still left his logic at home when he put on his evening clothes. If Irving chose to attract him to Shakespeare by lavish and spectacular revivals he was only showing his managerial acumen. "To succeed as an art the theatre must succeed as a business," was his motto. And the proof of the pudding was that he made Shakespeare, which had always spent financial disaster, pay. The accessories he lavished upon his productions, the authentic costumes, the incidental music by the foremost English composers, the designs by leading Royal Academicians, were to his audiences astonishingly beautiful. And if they counted for as much as Shakespeare's thought and poetry, the fault was not his. If he elected otherwise to appear in second-rate melodrama, it was because he was, first and foremost, an actor. He might have given the answer which his disciple Martin Harvey gave when similarly reproached: "My game is acting, and not necessarily the exploitation of literature. Material is chosen because it gives opportunities to practise my art—the art of acting." Moreover, as both these actors proved, that maligned species, melodrama, is a form of stage work into which, if artists engage in it, art may easily enter. It is perhaps even easier to be inventive and free in it than in the well-worn characters of older standing on the stage. There is a story of a famous French actor, who while rehearsing a new play noticed a worried look on the author's face. He stopped and asked him if he were dissatisfied. "*Vous n'ajoutez rien*," complained the author. The actor was adding nothing to the author's conception. To add was the art of acting. The actor may—indeed, he is expected to—add to melodrama; he adds to Shakespeare at his peril; he cannot add to Galsworthy and Shaw.

Lastly, when Irving began at the Lyceum where was he to find the new English drama to encourage? Arnold answered this question in his article in the *Nineteenth Century Review*. "In England," he wrote, "we have no modern drama at all. The time is not yet ripe for it." "Our vast society," he explained, "is not homogeneous enough, not sufficiently united, even any large portion of it, in a common view of life, a common ideal capable of serving as a basis for a modern English drama." It was clearly not to be found among the blank-verse closet playwrights, who deluged Irving with manuscripts. They were flogging a dead horse, imitating an obsolete dramatic form, which they knew only from the study. Nor was it to be sought for from the journeyman stage-authors who knew all the theatrical tricks but had long since ceased to draw on their invention. Of the coming playwrights of the 'nineties, Sydney Grundy was just beginning his career as a dramatist in the usual way as an adaptor of French plays; Arthur Pinero was an ardent first-night pittite with thoughts of becoming an actor and a few one-act farces in his head. Henry Arthur Jones was a commercial traveller, bombarding magazine editors with unwanted short stories. Oscar Wilde was still at school. When Irving tried to uplift the drama by opening the Lyceum to England's premier poet, the critics, said Archer, "went to be disappointed." They praised the actor's performance in what was really a minor part and faintly damned Tennyson's play.

When Irving wanted a new play as a change from Shakespeare and the old French melodrama, which had in their time served Jules Lemaitre and Charles Kean, he sensibly relied on the complaisant and industrious Wills, whose reputation stood so high that *The Hornet*, which, as its name implied, was not given to handing out compliments, once surprisingly referred to him as "the only living author whose work at all approaches that of the immortal Bard." His revisions of history were so idealistic, with the exception of his treatment of Oliver Cromwell and John Knox, that he was credited with contemplating the rehabilitation of Guy Fawkes.

The only dramatist who had been in the least creative excepting Robertson was W. S. Gilbert. In 1872 he had filled five London theatres though, apart from *Pygmalion and Galatea*, which owed much of its success to the charm and acting of Madge Robertson, the playwright's sister, his plays rarely reached the then average run of two hundred performances. Gilbert was recognized as a brilliant satirist, but his satire seemed to his contemporaries too brutal. It had too little of the element of good nature in it. As a writer of straight plays Gilbert must be pronounced a failure. It was not until he met Arthur Sullivan that he found his true *métier*. John Hollingshead was really the midwife of the partnership. In 1871 he put on Gilbert's *Thespis, or the Gods Grown Old* at the Gaiety. Sullivan, who had written the music, said: "I have never seen anything so beautifully put upon the stage." It only ran for a month and was soon forgotten by everybody but D'Oyly Carte. Carte wanted to do something very English, to create a form of light opera artistically and morally unobjectionable. This form of entertainment at this time was only represented by the French *opera bouffe*, of which the English adaptations were crude and unintelligent, and sometimes frankly improper. The composers who wrote the music for burlesque could not hold a candle to Offenbach and Lecoq. In 1875 D'Oyly Carte brought Gilbert and Sullivan together again, and the musician was persuaded to set the words of *Trial by Jury*, written years before. He produced it at the Royalty. Its success was instantaneous. There was now no escape for Sullivan from the famous partnership.

Of all the forms of dramatic art which Gilbert had attempted, and he had attempted practically everything, none was more congenial than burlesque. The ideas which flashed into his mind and obsessed him were always fantastic and paradoxical. He was naturally a mocker. But he had become disgusted with burlesque: the pointless punning, the unvaried jingling rhyme, the pantomime-dame and principal-boy convention, the focusing of the limelight on the actor, the gagging of the comedians, and the necessity of writing lyrics to familiar tunes. In *Thespis* he had already abandoned jingling rhyme for prose. He had already evolved in his mind a new form of comic opera which would discard all the vulgarities of burlesque and *opera bouffe*, in which, as G. K. Chesterton characteristically put it, "nothing incongruous should be permitted to mar the complete congruity of his own incongruity." He gagged the gaggers, insisted that original music should be written for his lyrics, and kept strictly within the bounds of a concentrated artistic unity. He could not quell the satirist within him, but he had learnt from the experience of his satiric comedies that criticism of his country or fellow-countrymen must be free from obvious malice and directness, that it was necessary to preserve the fiction that the objects of his criticism were foreigners or the people of some imaginary country, and to confine his satire to those faults which the Englishman is cheerfully willing to admit. And so in the Savoy operas he achieved what Chesterton called "the curious, half-unreal detachment in which some Victorians came at last to smile at all opinions including their own."

Among the audience shown in the illustration opposite there were the following:

1. Prince of Wales.
2. Princess of Wales.
3. C. Sykes, Esq.
4. Earl of Beaconsfield, K.G.
5. Montague Corry, Esq.
6. Edward Levy-Lawson, Esq.
7. Marquis of Hartington.
8. Right Hon. W. E. Gladstone.
9. Duchess of Sutherland.
10. Duchess of Manchester.
11. Duke of Sutherland.
12. Marquis of Salisbury, K.G.
13. Lord Carington.
14. H. Labouchere, Esq.
15. Cardinal Manning.
16. Edmund Yates, Esq.
17. Sergeant Ballantine.
18. Lord Dudley.
19. Lord Hardwicke.
20. Lady Dudley.
21. J. L. Toole, Esq.
22. Lionel Lawson, Esq.
23. Capt. F. Burnaby.
24. F. Leighton, P.R.A.
25. Val Prinsep, Esq.
26. Mrs Cornwallis West.
27. Mrs Langtry.
28. Lord Dunraven.
29. Sir John Bennett.
30. John Hollingshead, Esq.
31. Dion Boucicault, Esq.
32. Palgrave Simpson, Esq.
33. Lord Newry.
34. J. M. Posno, Esq.
35. J. E. Millais, Esq.
36. Lord Rosebery.
37. Lord A. Paget.
38. Douglas Straight, Esq.
39. Montague Williams, Esq.
40. H. J. Byron, Esq.
41. A. C. Swinburne, Esq.
42. F. C. Burnand, Esq.
43. Tom Taylor, Esq.
44. J. R. Planché, Esq.
45. Duke of Beaufort.
46. Lord Macduff.
47. G. A. Sala, Esq.
48. Baron Albert Grant.
49. Lord Ranelagh.
50. Earl Desart.
51. C. Sugden, Esq.
52. W. S. Gilbert, Esq.
53. A. Sullivan, Esq.
54. Wybrow Robertson, Esq.
55. S. Bancroft, Esq.
56. Archibald Forbes, Esq.
57. Count Batthyany.
58. Hon. O. Montague.
59. Marquess of Queensberry.
60. James Whistler, Esq.
61. Sir Henry de Bathe.
62. Lord Alington.
63. Sir Garnet Wolseley.
64. Col. J. Farquharson.
65. A. Borthwick, Esq.
66. Sir H. Hawkins.
67. Sir J. Holker.
68. Lord Dorchester.
69. Hon. Jas. Macdonald.
70. Col. Napier Sturt.
71. Dr William Russell.
72. Wilkie Collins, Esq.
73. Alfred Wigan, Esq.
74. Anthony Trollope, Esq.
75. J. Smith, Esq.
76. W. Brown, Esq.
77. John Parry, Esq.
78. Hon. S. Ponsonby Fane.
79. F. A. Marshall, Esq.
80. E. A. Sothern, Esq.
81. Sir Jules Benedict.
82. Sims Reeves, Esq.
83. Mr Herbert of Muckross.
84. S. Phelps, Esq.
85. Sir Geo. Wombwell.
86. J. C. Parkinson, Esq.
87. Lord Dupplin.
88. Lord C. Beresford.
89. Lord H. Lennox.
90. Sir Robert Peel.
91. G. Lewis, Esq.
92. Henry Irving, Esq.

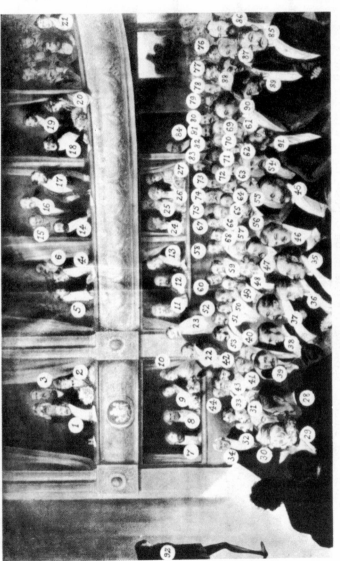

AN IRVING FIRST NIGHT

See opposite page for key.

THE CORSICAN BROTHERS.

IRVING OUTDOES HIMSELF

FABIEN. "I must congratulate you! The very best
performance I have ever seen."
LOUIS. "After yours, my dear sir. After yours."

From the Gabrielle Enthoven Collection; by courtesy of the Victoria and Albert Museum

IV

AURORA BOREALIS

The Eighteen-eighties

AT the end of the eighteen-seventies a gradual change was taking place in the constitution of theatre audiences. At that time every kind of entertainment was patronized by the same body of habitual playgoers. Units of the same regular crowd whose applause ensured the success of a Shakespeare play would go the following night to a trumpery burlesque or revisit H. J. Byron's perennial farce *Our Boys*, which opened in 1875 and ran for four-and-a-half years. Its record of 1362 performances remained unbroken till Chu Chin Chow. Its popularity was so phenomenal that the Strand omnibuses pulled up outside the Vaudeville and the conductors shouted "Our Boys." This regular playgoing public, to whom the theatre was just the theatre, was being increasingly recruited from the wealthier classes. Though there was a strong feeling in the West End clubs when the price of a stall rose to ten shillings, every one insisted on sitting in the stalls, where a white tie and tails were now *de rigueur*. Raised prices did not deter them. They readily paid a guinea to see Irving and Edwin Booth act together in 1881. Private boxes yawned emptily. The upper boxes went begging and were given away to small shopkeepers, who exhibited the large bills of the theatre on their area railings. The dress circle (frock or morning coat) was difficult to fill and had to be papered with complimentary

81

tickets, usually circulated in the suburbs and lodging-house districts around Russell Square. Their holders, according to W. S. Gilbert, could easily be recognized by the persistence with which they sucked acidulated drops throughout the performance. Though the dress-circle seats were half the price of the stalls, aristocratic visitors would have none of them. The Holborn Theatre even introduced an undress circle.

A change was also taking place in the class of those who patronized the pit. It was significant that in 1878 at the Court Theatre, of which John Hare had become the lessee in 1875, bringing with him the genteel traditions of the Prince of Wales's, for the first time ices and coffee were handed round the pit in the intervals instead of the customary oranges and ginger-beer. The pit had long been pampered in that it had, at a nominal cost, enjoyed the best seats in the house. In some of the older theatres they were, in fact, the only seats in which it was possible to see and hear and breathe. The pittites, for the most part trained and critical *habitués*, who, as lovers of the drama for the drama's sake, considered it their self-appointed duty to give a broad and unmistakeable verdict of approval or condemnation, and had become used to being flatteringly regarded as the fountain head of dramatic taste and appreciation, now suddenly found their prerogative threatened by the rising tide of the stalls. They were first pushed back. Then, in some theatres, crowded out altogether and relegated to an upper circle. When the Bancrofts took over and reconstructed the Haymarket in 1880 they abolished the pit. Though this oligarchical revolution was for economical reasons inevitable sooner or later, it was the occasion of violent first-night demonstrations by the disappointed pittites. Clement Scott came forward as their champion. He declared magnificently that the seats of "the best friends of the drama" were being handed over to "the professors of a scented dilettantism," late-comers in evening dress (a fashion which began at the Lyceum) who came to the theatre from pure idleness and were unpunctual, restless, and talkative. They arrived fresh from dinner with loosened tongues, babbled to each other during the performance, and left disturbingly before the curtain to go on to a supper party. From now on the feeding-habits of the upper classes had a considerable influence on the nature of dramatic fare.

The Battle for the Pit went on for about ten years. Even in 1886 malcontents still mustered on first nights outside the Haymarket to air their grievance. Managers tried to compensate them by greater comfort in their new quarters by giving them upholstered seats with backs. Irving, on his return from the United States in 1884, attempted to introduce the reservation of seats for the pit, but the pittites indignantly protested. Finally, in most theatres a restricted and more comfortable pit resulted; but many of the disgruntled pittites deserted the theatre for the music-hall, and the pit in consequence became less preponderantly masculine. The change in the constitution of the audience led to a change from the old triple bill. First the after-piece dropped out, and then gradually the curtain-raiser as well. Four, then three, acts became the normal division of the play; the play began later and the playing time was shortened. The Bancrofts at the Prince of Wales's had exceptionally succeeded in making the 'swells' dine earlier and take their seats at 7.45, but the late dining habit of the upper classes was hard to break, and at most other houses the first part of the programme catered for the pit and gallery. With a programme adjusted to their convenience the stalls learnt manners, and the art of acting did not, as Clement Scott had prophesied, suffer from the insolent inattention of the usurpers of the pit.

By the mid-eighties the play-going public was beginning to divide itself into three main categories: the naïvely un-questioning, who uncritically accepted what they saw as real life, or, coming jaded from the impure air of shops, factories, and offices, from the hard stress of business, pro-fessional, and domestic duties, were incapable or impatient of the intellectual exertion or the prolonged attention necessary to judge a serious work of art; secondly, an advanced, constant, educated section, eager for a serious drama which would attempt to interpret life; and thirdly, a ribald, sneering section, ingenious in extracting mirth from scenes meant to be pathetic, who came not to be amused, touched, or interested, but to show their superiority to the poor deluded fools who *were* amused, touched, and interested.

This was the opinion of that keen observer of popular reaction to the play, Henry Arthur Jones, the prophet of the new English drama. It was evidently time for the theatre to segregate these incongruous elements and to cater for them separately. This is precisely what happened. The new generation of theatre-managers, composed increasingly of actors who managed their own theatres, began more and more to adopt a settled policy, to create their own special audiences by imposing on them their taste and personality. Though they were still conservative in their choice of plays and, to a great extent, followed the safe line of revivals and adaptations from the French, they were quietly and permanently educating their audiences by the high standard of their productions. The theatre advances quite as much through the excellence in staging and acting of popular plays as through the insistence upon the literary quality of plays which cannot be popular. And now there was a marked advance all along the line. Under the guid-ance of these actor-managers the public became less tolerant of rough humour and broad caricature, more fastidious as

takes the blame upon himself, the forged note is stolen from the villain who is in love with Nora and destroyed, and all ends happily. In 1889 *The Doll's House*, unadulterated, was put on by Charles Carrington and his wife, Janet Achurch, for seven performances, extended to twenty-one. The average receipts were £35–45, and £70 of their £100 capital was lost. Not more than three thousand persons can have seen it; yet it brought to the boil a critical battle which had been simmering since 1880. Before the publication of William Archer's *English Dramatists of To-day* in 1882 there had been practically no attempt at theoretical dramatic criticism. Critics had habitually contented themselves and their editors with theatrical reporting; they announced the title of a new play, revealed its plot, and gave a good-natured opinion on the merits of the performers. Consequently the old-school critic was more interested in, and by training a better judge of, the actor than the play. But a new school was growing up to whom the play was the all-important thing. The function of dramatic criticism had been defined for them by Matthew Arnold. It was not "to make adverse remarks about plays that happen to be bad"—he added a warning against the prevalent temptation of the dramatic critic: facetiousness—but "to discover what is best in current drama and to teach the public what is best by making clear the reasons why." The new criticism must be empirical, not deductive; its principles obtained inductively. By a disinterested endeavour to learn and propagate the best that is known and thought in the theatre of the world, it should be possible to establish a current of fresh and true ideas. The new critic inevitably sought his principles on the Continent, set buzzing by the 'realism' of Ibsen and the 'naturalism' of Zola, and thus became the champion of what was called the Theatre of Ideas.

The production of *The Doll's House* crystallized the conflict. Ancients and Moderns ranged themselves in two opposing camps behind their leaders, Clement Scott and William Archer. Scott stuck obstinately to his stereotyped formulæ: the playwright's business was to tell a story, not to treat his audience to "scraps of philosophy, shreds of essays, and rent garments of social ethics." Archer fought for a drama which would open intellectual, moral, and political questions; for a stimulating and not a sedative drama; for "a body of playwrights, however small, whose works are not only acted, but printed and read." His followers indisciminately reviled every form of unintellectual drama. They slated with equal vehemence the "strong" drama, the well-made play, burlesque, and farce, and barely concealed their contempt for the actor-manager who countenanced these plays and acted in them. In writing of Ibsen the *mot d'ordre* was unequivocal: mud-sling or rave. The Moderns put in a few extra ecstatic adjectives to meet the excess of abuse anticipated from the other side; the Ancients hit harder than they felt the truth demanded in order to get a fair hearing. When it came to dealing with Jones and Pinero, independently striving for an intellectual and literary drama according to their lights, the Moderns were in something of a dilemma. The itch to pooh-pooh them had to be tempered tactfully in order to detect in them the influence of the Master. They had to give them faint praise as being "a step in the right direction" while the Ancients gibed at the Moderns' impudent assertion that any braver handling of the stuff of life must of course be due to the illuminating rays of "our new star of the North."

When *The Doll's House* let loose a storm of moral indignation from the Ancients, the Married Woman's Property Act was seven years old. The National Society for Women's Suffrage had been founded three years before. Girton and

Newnham were flourishing institutions. To-day it seems absurd that any one should really have been shocked by Ibsen's play. It was at that time, however, rather the fashion to be shocked, and Ibsen's vociferous opponents led the public to believe that he was disgusting and immoral. Scott coined the word "ibscene." Poor Nora's phrase and Dr Rank's answer about the stockings caused a shudder among worthy folk, who had laughed at farces centring round a pair of corsets and had gazed at leagues of stocking-less legs without a blush. When J. T. Grein put on *Ghosts* at a technically private performance at the Royalty in 1891, after it had been banned by the Censor, the outcry, of course, redoubled. But although curiosity drew many people to Toole's tiny theatre at Charing Cross to see the popular comedian, made up with bushy whiskers to look like Ibsen, in J. M. Barrie's maiden dramatic effort, a burlesque called *Ibsen's Ghost*, the general public was not really interested to find out whether the much-debated Scandinavian dramatist was a subversive propagandist or an incomparable artist. In that superficial way it has of picking up a cliché to dispose of any new controversial topic it made up its mind that Ibsen was horrid, and even worse, suburban. It was not concerned about the social amplitude he had given to the "useful" theatre of Dumas Fils and Augier. The prosperous and contented middle-class theatre-goer liked his *dramatis personæ* to be drawn from the best society. His womenfolk went to the theatre as much for the dresses as the drama, and read in *The Queen* the first night description of the gowns worn on the stage more avidly than the dramatic criticisms. What mattered to them was that Ibsen's characters were dowdy—to say nothing of the fact that they were informed by *The Saturday Review*, the superior person's stand-by, that his plays were "written in order to satirize the detested middle classes," to which they belonged. They could smile with a serene detachment at that witty Mr Gilbert's barbs fictitiously aimed at the inhabitants of some foreign or imaginary country, but forceful and militant satire was surely not quite in good taste. The time for that had not arrived. One English playwright had attempted it. H. A. Jones's *Saints and Sinners*, a malicious satire on the hypocritical, chapel-going, tradesman milieu in which he was brought up, was produced in 1884, the year Spurgeon declared that a playgoer ceased *ipso facto* to be a member of a Christian community and the playwright saccharined *The Doll's House* for popular consumption. Admiration for the audacity of *Saints and Sinners* vies with amazement at the author's lack of understanding for Ibsen. Jones's play, now generally regarded as a landmark in the history of the modern English drama, raised an immediate storm of protest at its "religious blasphemies" because he allowed his tradesmen to quote scripture to their purpose. Jones sent his brother-in-law to the pit on the first night to gauge the feeling of that important section of the audience. He sat next to a leading member of the Playgoers' Club, founded that year, a band of earnest students of the drama, whom Jones had encouraged and supported, and who considered themselves as the advance guard of an enlightened public *in esse*. At each scriptural quotation this pioneer hissed vigorously, and remarked: "I hope they'll show Jones that they won't stand trifling with sacred things."

The new dramatist, eager to advance towards a more thoughtful drama and to extend the range of subjects permissible for treatment on the stage, had to progress very gingerly. The advance began four years later, and however timid in expounding a real philosophy of life, the bolder spirits did try to debate phenomena of social rather than individual interest. But the prime influence was not Ibsen it was still the French serious drama with its melodramatic tendencies and its conventional *dénouement*, in which virtue was extolled, if not rewarded, and vice censured, if not punished. If audiences were not properly susceptible to any implied challenge to orthodoxy or decorum the *Daily Telegraph* was always there to admonish them with firm and steadfast morality. Life on the stage was still as improper as the Nude in art. In 1894 H. A. Jones had to write a *Preface to Mrs Grundy* to his published edition of *The Case of Rebellious Susan* and Aubrey Beardsley noted on some proofs of the first state of an illustration to *Salome:*

> Because this figure was undressed
> This little drawing was suppressed.
> It was unkind, but never mind,
> Perhaps it was all for the best.

Of the two pioneers of the new drama of social significance precedence must be given to Henry Arthur Jones. He was far bolder than A. W. Pinero. He did not hesitate to attack the hypocrites and Philistines, the busybody philanthropists, the ruthless employers of labour, the imposters who exploited mental healing and prophecy, social shams, and superstitions. But his progress was necessarily two steps forward and one step back. He alternated his social satires with sentimental pot-boilers; excusably, because the latter were popular and the former almost invariably booed by the first-night audience, trounced by the critics, and rapidly withdrawn. "The melancholy truth," wrote Bernard Shaw after the failure of *Michael and His Lost Angel* in 1896, which ran for eleven nights, "is that the English stage got a good play, and was completely and ignominiously beaten by it. Mr Jones has got beyond the penny novelist conditions which are actable in our theatres."

Pinero was far more wary. He first quitted the field of farce and sentimental comedy, which had won him recog-

nition as a craftsman of exceptional ability with *The Profligate*, the opening play of John Hare's first season of management at the Garrick in 1889. Hare's faithful audience, which
had followed him in his peregrinations, flocked to the
theatre in a mood of critical curiosity—in view of the
rumours about the play—rather than with the usual pleasurable anticipation. The play was lachrymose and gloomy,
but there were no boos. Pinero had "handled a difficult
subject with remarkable delicacy," which meant that he
had played safe. *The Doll's House* might mistakenly be
interpreted as an incitement to the *femme incomprise* to leave
her home and babies, but the moral of *The Profligate*—that
a man who has been false to one woman has no right to the
love of a second—if not even then generally accepted, was
unexceptionable. The French social drama had prepared
the way for the treatment, if not the discussion, of problems
of sexual morality, particularly the position of the ladies of
the *demi-monde* which, as Dumas Fils explained, meant not
la cohue des courtisanes but *la classe de déclassées*. Pinero was
not out to propound a new moral code. He was a professional playwright, wise enough to accept his manager's
suggestion of an amended happy ending, shrewd enough to
present ideas on a rising market. There was just sufficient
daring about *The Second Mrs Tanqueray* and *The Notorious
Mrs Ebbsmith* to scandalize very mildly those who saw it
and to make those who had not seen it all the more eager
to do so.

Woman—the wronged wife, the woman with a past, the
New Woman—dominated the theatre in the early 'nineties.
What a boon she was to rising actresses! But Mrs Grundy
was ever on the alert. Her vigilance was responsible for
many stage suicides or alternatively illogical happy endings.
She frowned on any suggestion of the possibility of redemption for the woman who had once defied moral convention

or that the Wild Oats theory was permissible to the weaker sex. There was no imitation on the stage of Grant Allen's scandalous novel *The Woman who Did*. When in *The Case of Rebellious Susan* (1894) Jones implied that what was sauce for the gander might be sauce for the goose by stating explicitly that his heroine had paid out her unfaithful husband in his own coin, the leading actor refused to utter the lines that made this clear.

However circumscribed the treatment allowed the dramatist by Mrs Grundy, the emergence of the term 'problem play' indicated a new conception of the purpose of the drama. The term, invented by the unrepentantly old-fashioned Sydney Grundy and tauntingly flung at the Intellectual Theatre, attached itself to the matrimonial drama. But it was not particularly apt. These plays were not really problem plays at all, or, at any rate, such problems as were raised, one knew beforehand, would be solved with strict conventionality. Religious or sociological questions were still taboo. The public, squeamish on moral questions, was bored by sociology. "Sociology is too complex, too much in the air, too tedious for treatment in a serious spirit on the stage," wrote the *Athenæum* in explanation of the failure of a strike play, *The People's Idol* (1890), produced by Wilson Barrett for his opening at the New Olympic, sixteen years in advance of Galsworthy's *Strife*. The reviewer admitted that the author had handled his problem with reasonable argument, but explained: "The middle class embraces its prejudices and loves not argument. The lower class—the great residuum who enjoy the courtesy title of 'working men'—hates reason." Six years later the paper repeated its assertion that "in the present condition it is unlikely that any serious play—of seriously intellectual interest—dealing with any problem of sociology in a serious spirit can live on the English stage." It may be deduced that theatre audiences were not yet ready to think. What chance had *Widowers' Houses* in 1892, a first play by an unsuccessful novelist who had recently joined in the attack upon the theatre and conventional religion in a paper read before the Church and Stage Guild in which "in the most sweet-natured of fashions he said the most shocking and hazardous things about both." The banning of *Mrs Warren's Profession* was, of course, a foregone conclusion.

For the time being the odds were too heavy against the Intellectual Theatre. The most it could do was to elevate the melodrama adventuress in the social scale and make nonsense of any problem in a superfluous fourth act. Even the temporary vogue for the society matrimonial drama did not last. In 1884 Sidney Grundy, who, knowing which side his bread was buttered, had stuck to mere entertainment and the Scribe-Labiche-Sardou formulae, instanced the failure of all profoundly didactic plays and the success of nearly everything light and amusing. In 1895 Jones optimistically published his *Renascence of the English Drama*, but it was little more than wishful thinking, for in the following year the failure of the serious playwright to consolidate his position was evident. Jones himself was so much on the defensive as to admit: "The wise statesman does not attempt to make laws too far in advance of the moral and intellectual condition of the people. Nor does the wise playwright forget that playwriting is very rigorously limited in similar respects. Play-writing prospers only by virtue of immediately pleasing a large section of the public. If it does not do this it has no *raison d'être* whatever." The problem of uniting the demands of an audience insisting on amusement with the demands of an art looking beyond amusement remained therefore unsolved. It could not be done by representing Life as founded on the experience of a so-called cultivated society dwelling between Chelsea and Hampstead, or by a conservative treatment of such wearisome themes as the difficulty of legitimizing a love affair illegitimate to start with. In 1897 Jones gave up the struggle and turned to high comedy with *The Liars*. Pinero followed suit in 1898 with *The Gay Lord Quex*. And everybody was happy.

For a time the theatre's attack of intellectual measles had seriously threatened the livelihood of the actor and actress who specialized in comedy. To a letter written to Mrs John Wood in 1894, regretting her absence from the stage, the comedienne replied: "It's not my fault I've not acted. It's the authors who are to blame. They won't be funny and they are driving me to tradegy. I can't even spell the word, how shall I act it?"

Meanwhile the Robertsonian sentimental comedy had burst into a sudden reblossoming. Haddon Chambers's *John o' Dreams*, quite unashamedly romantic, was greeted as "a whiff of fresh sea air after the wearisome so-called problem plays and impossibly tiresome domestic drama." J. M. Barrie's *The Professor's Love Story* pained Archer as being "a calculated disloyalty to art," but ran for five hundred performances. *Charley's Aunt* and *The New Boy* "teach no lesson and pretend to teach none. They are not problem plays, they are not psychological," declared the *Saturday Review* a year before G.B.S. accepted the post of dramatic critic. The stage was suddenly deluged with adaptations from popular novels and the succession of musical comedies which followed *The Geisha* and, said A. B. Walkley, "snuffed out the Savoy opera." Even the "gilded philosophic pill" had grown unpalatable. In 1897 J. T. Grein, embittered by the lack of support for his Independent Theatre, in an article in the *Revue de l'Art Dramatique*, informing French readers about the condition of the drama in England, sadly observed: "*C'est—force nous est de le reconnaitre—l'apothéose honteuse et dégradante du système commercial.*"

Nevertheless in these years of apparent retrogression the work of the crusaders, now aided by the caustic pen of the new dramatic critic of the *Saturday Review*, was bearing unseen fruit. The leaven of Ibsenism was gradually leavening the lump. Slowly the influence of his consummate and revolutionary technique was infiltrating and superseding the technique of the well-made play. Five of his plays were staged. In 1896 three of London's leading actresses, Janet Achurch (the first English Nora), Elizabeth Robins (the first Hedda Gabler), and Mrs Patrick Campbell appeared together in four matinées of *Little Eyolf*. From then on the intelligent woman takes her place in the vanguard of the forward march of the theatre. How did *Little Eyolf* strike an open-minded theatre-lover in 1896? *The Sketch* published a letter from *One of the Gods*, which gives us a very fair idea.

I have read the opinion of many critics that Ibsen's plays are 'balderdash.' I don't quite know what balderdash means, but it is a mighty fine word and it made me very desirous of acquainting myself with Mr Ibsen's plays. So when I saw that three of our best actresses were producing *Little Eyolf* I left my afternoon's work and paid my shilling for a seat in the gallery. Well, honestly, it seemed to me a strange sort of play. I felt rather 'fogged' over the first act. Yet when the curtain fell I knew I wanted to see the second act badly; and when the second act closed I felt more interested than ever in the third; and when *that* was over and the lights turned out, and the people hastened away—well, I wanted to go straight home and think it over. I have been thinking it over ever since, and the only conclusion I can arrive at is that 'balderdash' is a mighty fine word, *Little Eyolf* a mighty fine play, but the gentleman who used the word didn't know its meaning.

A COCHRAN FIRST NIGHT
Pearl Binder
By courtesy of the artist

"AFTER YOURS, MY DEAR SIR" : MODERN VERSION

John Gielgud and Laurence Olivier in *Romeo and Juliet*

This exactly explains the novelty as well as the peculiar fascination of Ibsen's technique. The Victorian playgoer was accustomed to a preliminary exposition—the butler informing the housemaid as they dusted the furniture that their master's financial position was precarious and that he was trying to find a rich husband for his daughter, who was in love with her music-teacher, etc.—and to an immediate clarification, by means of asides and soliloquies, of the motives of the actions of the characters. Naturally he was fogged by a play which was only made comprehensible as it proceeded; in which the second act cleared up the mystifications of the first, and the final illumination was reserved for the last scene. It was like having to learn a new language with a syntax similar to German, in which the verb only makes its appearance at the end of the sentence, and without it the sentence is unintelligible. But once the playgoer had learnt to understand the new dramatic language, it was goodbye to asides, soliloquies, and opening expositions. Imperceptibly Ibsen had altered the style and method, the very conception of the drama in the minds of many dramatists, and these changes demanded and received a greater effort of concentration from audiences. In the course of his long campaigning for an intellectual and literary drama Henry Arthur Jones made a number of optimistic and barely justifiable generalizations, but one of them was true.

The public taste is modifiable within very wide limits. The public may be led almost anywhere, easily and temporarily, to any kind of new sensation or falsity, strenuously but permanently to the appreciation of what is of lasting worth. One hears constantly an outcry against the foolishness to trying to educate the public in matters of amusement, but all the while a very real education is going on amongst us.

The Ibsen episode was to bear its fruit in the next decade.

V

CYCLONES AND ANTICYCLONES

The Eighteen-nineties

UP till 1891 very few playwrights published their plays with the exception of those poetic dramatists who wrote for the study and not for the stage. The lax American copyright law gave no protection to published plays. D'Oyly Carte, made wise by unfortunate experiences with the earlier Gilbert and Sullivan operas, had to preserve the very title of *Iolanthe* a secret till the eleventh hour in order to thwart piracy on the other side of the Atlantic by simultaneous production here and in America. But one of the results of the Anglo-American Copyright Law of 1891 was the publication of reading editions of plays, shorn of the detailed stage directions that disfigure acting editions for the layman, and sometimes with the addition of prefaces. It was only natural that the playwright, once he was able to address a reading public as well as a theatre-audience, should be at pains to add a literary quality to his work. This was all to the good. By publishing his plays he invited a second judgment on them, not as a man of the theatre, but as a man of letters. In his desire to pass this test he may excusably have been inclined to make his dialogue too literary. A certain pompousness crept into the colloquial style. There is a stodginess in the Society dramas of the early 'nineties due as much to their language as to their moralizing tendency.

The drama had begun perhaps to take itself a little too

seriously. Can one to-day quite imagine the delight of being suddenly presented, after a steady diet of very English pudding, with an *omelette surprise*? *The Importance of Being Earnest* has come to occupy a unique place in dramatic literature, and has possibly led the dramatic historian into over-rating Oscar Wilde's merits as a playwright, even to the extent of attributing a natural development towards a more literary comedy to his specific influence.

The moderate success of Wilde's first social drama, *Lady Windermere's Fan*, owed much to the excellence of the acting and the notoriety of the already notorious author's behaviour when he made his first-night curtain speech smoking a cigarette and congratulating the audience upon their, not his, success. "The public," he explained in a subsequent interview, "makes a success when it realizes that a play is a work of art." The implication that his play was a work of art was sheer impertinence. But impertinence was his strong suit. He had earned a reputation by it. It is much easier to be impertinent than funny, and it goes down twice as well with people of refinement. His plots were as old-fashioned as his knee-breeches and his affectation of an out-moded dandyism. They were also second-hand, like his early poetry, Swinburne and water. The stale devices on which they hinged—the dropped fan, the stolen letter, the indiscreet wife concealed from her jealous husband, the surprise revelation of a hidden identity—dated back to, and beyond, the well-made play: to Scribe, to Dumas Père, to Sheridan. His characters were stock puppets, who all talked like one another; but for their salvation they all talked like Oscar Wilde. He gave these threadbare, borrowed props a semblance of freshness by spangling them with the sequins of his coruscating dinner-table wit. Wilde once asked Ouida the secret of her popularity. "I am the only novelist," she replied, "who knows how two Dukes talk when they are together." Wilde persuaded his audience that he was the only playwright who knew how two Duchesses talk when they are together. This flattered the duchesses, who were happy to believe they talked like Oscar Wilde, as well as the commoners, who were enchanted at being admitted into such scintillating society. And, unused to wit in the theatre except at the Savoy, they laughed conscientiously at every epigram. "Each person," wrote Shaw in the *Saturday Review*, "comes to the theatre prepared, like a special artist, with the background of a laugh ready sketched in his or her features."

Wilde did not choose the dramatic form because it was a necessity of his nature, regardless of whether or not his plays ever reached the stage, as did Swinburne and Alfred de Musset, and as he did himself exceptionally when he wrote *Salome*. He turned to the theatre because he needed to make money; because other forms of literary work, even if they had enhanced his reputation, had failed to make him financially independent. He had already tried his hand at play-writing soon after he came down from Oxford without showing any natural aptitude for the theatre. *Vera, or the Nihilists*, written in 1881, the year of the assassination of the Tsar Alexander II (and incidentally of *Patience*) was a conventional melodrama with a topical flavour. It was a very bad one. Announced for production at the Adelphi, it was cancelled during rehearsal, ostensibly on the grounds that the author was dissatisfied with the rendition of the cast. It was, however, staged two years later in New York and was deservedly a fiasco. His second attempt, commissioned for Mary Anderson when Wilde was in the United States in 1882, *The Duchess of Padua*, a five-act tragedy, was only another melodrama bedecked with the feathers of Elizabethan blank verse. Miss Anderson refused to appear in it.

This instinctive tendency to derivative melodrama must be remarked because in view of *The Importance of Being Earnest* one might be inclined to think that he wrote his melodramatic social dramas, with their well-chosen titles in the fashion of the moment, with his tongue in his cheek. But that was clearly not the case. He believed in the originality of his hackneyed plots and stale theatrical devices as fervently as any purveyor of Drury Lane melodrama. In his notes for the draft of *An Ideal Husband* he makes the marginal comment on the stealing of Lady Chiltern's letter: "An excellent idea!" as if it had never been used before. He spoke of Mrs Erlynne as "a character as yet untouched in literature." He resisted experienced advice from George Alexander and treated his actor-manager's suggestions with contempt. He was no better in this respect than Cecil Raleigh, the author of a succession of Drury Lane melodramas, who took himself with such deadly earnest that he refused to alter a line that he had written until finally Arthur Collins lost patience and did the rewriting himself, as Alexander practically had to do with the end of the second act of *Lady Windermere's Fan*.

Despite the individuality of their sparkling dialogue, there is in Wilde's three social dramas no originality and only second-rate craftsmanship. To suggest that they were works of art was either impudence or obliquity of judgment. There was nothing in them except the epigrams to prepare for *The Importance of Being Earnest*, which seems the uniquely original play of the century. But how far was it original?

When the play appeared in 1895 a critic observed: "The mantle of Mr Gilbert has fallen on the shoulders of Mr Oscar Wilde, who wears it in the jauntiest fashion." Was this allusion to W. S. Gilbert merely a superficial comparison, the critical urge to discover a line of succession, or did the play subconsciously remind the writer of a specific play

of Gilbert's? Subconsciously, because then the Gilbert of
the Savoy operas had eclipsed the Gilbert of the 'seventies.
His satirical comedies were barely, if at all, remembered in
the 'nineties. There is no evidence that Wilde saw acted
Gilbert's short-lived play, *Engaged*. It seems probable that
he did because it was produced in the year in which Wilde
was writing his own first play. If not, he could have read
it, for it was included in a collection of Gilbert's straight
plays published in 1881. At all events the resemblances
between *Engaged* and *The Importance of Being Earnest* are
too remarkable to have been mere coincidence, and it is as
astonishing that no one appears to have pointed them out
as it is that Wilde should not earlier have recognized the
affinity of his special talent for cynical witticism with that
of W. S. Gilbert.

The attitude, the spirit, of both plays is the same. Contemporary critical opinion used the same words of each.
Gilbert's "heartless cynicism" offended the public of 1877;
Wilde's "absolute heartlessness" delighted the public of
1895. The two plays were alike in their unrestrained
absurdity—for example, Miss Prism's injunction to her
pupil to read her Political Economy, "omitting the chapter
on the Fall of the Rupee as somewhat too sensational."
They were alike in exposing the very practical material
considerations which underlie the sentimental pose of the
young ladies in the play, especially the frank utterance of
their true feelings. Compare Lady Bracknell's questioning
of Jack Worthing preparatory to entering his name on her
list of eligibles, "should his answers be what a really affec-
tionate mother requires," with Belinda's asking her lover
Belawney for a statement as to the permanence of his
income. Belinda's "I love you madly, passionately; yet
before I consent to take the irrevocable step that will place
me on the pinnacle of my fondest hopes, you must give me

some definite idea of your financial position" finds an echo in the tone of Gwendolen's "Although she may prevent us from becoming man and wife, and I may marry some one else, and marry often, nothing she can possibly do will alter my eternal devotion to you."

The resemblance is even closer. There are parallel scenes. In *Engaged* the two girls, Belinda and Minnie, both wish to marry Cheviot; in fact Belinda believes she is already married to him, the validity of their impromptu wedding being however in doubt because they are uncertain whether it took place on the Scottish or the English side of the border. They meet as Minnie, in ignorance of this ceremony, is preparing for her wedding to the man Belinda believes to be her husband. Some refreshments are laid out on the buffet. Similarly, Gwendolen and Cecily, rivals for a still undetermined Ernest, meet at the tea-table. The scene in Act II of *The Importance of Being Earnest*—the initial gushing friendliness gradually changing to hostility and then to a sisterly compact when they learn of the deception practised upon them—proceeds on exactly the same lines as the scene between Belinda and Minnie, who, after the same preliminary skirmishes, conclude their reconciliation as follows:

BELINDA: Minnie, if dear Cheviot should prove to be my husband, swear to me that that will not prevent your coming to stay with us—with dear Cheviot and me—whenever you can.

MINNIE: Indeed I will. And if it should turn out that dear Cheviot is at liberty to marry me, promise me that that will not prevent your looking on our house—dear Cheviot's and mine—as your home.

BELINDA: I swear it. We will be like dear, dear sisters.

The symmetrical construction of Gilbert's dialogue, its antiphonal arrangement, obvious even in this quotaton, is imitated in Wilde's exquisitely patterned comedy. And during the first part of this scene in which Minnie and Belinda spar as cattishly as Gwendolen and Cecily, Belinda infuriates her rival by eating tarts from the wedding buffet, a piece of comic business used twice in *The Importance of Being Earnest*, first with cucumber sandwiches and then again with muffins.

Later in Gilbert's play the bridegroom Cheviot, in the dilemma of not knowing whether he is still a bachelor or about to become a bigamist, and also in the belief that he is financially ruined, threatens to commit suicide. Before the audience knows whether he has carried out this threat Symperson, Minnie's father, enters in deep mourning, just as Jack Worthing does after the supposed demise of his imaginary brother. When Cheviot comes back to inform him that he has changed his mind and consented to live, Symerson indignantly protests:

> Consented to live? Why, sir, this is confounded trifling. I don't understand this line of conduct at all; you threaten to commit suicide; your friends are dreadfully shocked at first, but eventually their minds become reconciled to the prospect of losing you, they become resigned, even cheerful; and when they have brought themselves to this Christian state of mind, you coolly inform them that you have changed your mind and mean to live. It's not business, sir—it's not business.

The tone is exactly the same as Algernon's: "Relations are simply a tedious pack of people who haven't got the remotest knowledge of how to live, nor the smallest instinct when to die," and Lady Bracknell's unmoved comment when she is told that Bunbury is dead: "I am glad that he made up his mind at the last to some definite course of action, and acted under proper medical advice." Nobody could possibly say any of these things. They are funny because of their absurdity and utter callousness. And this is the keynote of both plays.

Finally, in a preliminary note to the published edition of *Engaged* Gilbert wrote: "It is absolutely essential to the success of this piece that it should be played with the most perfect earnestness and gravity throughout." In other words, he stressed the importance of being earnest.

It is very difficult to believe that all these resemblances were just coincidental, almost as difficult as it is to believe that Wilde wrote his light-hearted comedy in a month, as he claimed to have done, at a time when he had financial and other even more serious worries on his mind. It is more credible that in those weeks he should have put the final polish on a play long pondered and first suggested by Gilbert's forgotten *Engaged*. Wilde's comedy is the more finished of the two; it stands unrivalled. One would call it the most original comedy in the English language, were it not for the fact that the originality is suspiciously like Gilbert's. What is interesting is the disappearance in the theatre public of that sentimentality which had been outraged by Gilbert's "cruel heartlessness."

Bernard Shaw's notice of *The Importance of Being Earnest* deserves quotation:

> There is a scene between the two girls in the second act quite in the manner of Mr Gilbert and almost inhuman enough to have been written by him. . . . The general effect is that of a farcical comedy dating from the 'seventies, unplayed during that period because it was too clever and too decent, and brought up to date as far as possible by Mr Wilde in his now completely formed style. . . . I must decline to accept it as a day less than ten years old.

The cynical mockery of the romantic conception of love and marriage, of the lingering Tupperism of the mid-

Victorian age, which was found distasteful in 1877 and deliciously piquant in 1895, heralded an age of irreverence and ridicule: ridicule of the things which had been cherished convictions of the previous generation and which it was only beginning to outgrow. For Romance still had another decade of life. Unblushing sentiment was still a trump card if rightly played. J. M. Barrie with the unerring cleverness of the perceptive child played it unblushingly and triumphantly in 1894. *The Professor's Love Story*, despite its near-puerility, entranced five hundred audiences. Grave gentlemen, brought up in the British public-school tradition of unemotionalism, who had grown into Mr Dombeys or were growing into Soames Forsytes, were surprised—perhaps not unpleasantly—to find themselves blowing their noses. Graduates of Girton who, like Miss Bell Golightly, that travesty of the New Woman in Barrie's previous play, *Walker, London*, professed to believe that love was purely intellectual (all other love being founded on an entological misconception) discovered, as did that lady, that they were conventionally feminine. *Fin de siècle* audiences were still unsure of themselves. They still secretly resented being made to think instead of feel inside the theatre. Not yet acclimatized to the bracing ozone of the intellectual theatre, they privately preferred the relaxing air of sentimental comedy. W. L. Courtney gives this recipé for the then acceptable play: "There must be a little psychological analysis, but not too much; a little girding at social conventions, but social conventions must ultimately prevail; there must not be too much logic, but there must be romance and sentiment."

It was not unnatural that Queen Victoria's Jubilee should have made people nostalgic. It was an excuse to call a temporary halt to the too rapid march of time, to banish the bogey of Ibsenism from the theatre. *Hearts are Trumps* was the significant title of a play of 1899. It stands as representative of a spate of romantic sentimental plays: *Trilby, The Little Minister, The Adventure of Lady Ursula, The Only Way*, etc., that flooded the stage at the close of the century; the counter-current to the rising tide of realism. Even Shaw's Pleasant Plays were dressed in romantic fashion.

Romance was an antidote to the increasing utilitarianism of life; sentiment a relief from the cult of the poker face. The repressions of nature always seek an outlet in the theatre. The conventional display of feminine 'understandings' in burlesque, which led a French critic to observe that the English would rather see an actress in tights than in parts doubtless had its origin as a relief to Puritan repression. But as far as the stage was concerned the Naughty Nineties was a misnomer. Burlesque was dead, and with it the semi-nudity which had increasingly debased it. By modern standards it was probably not very indecorous, though E. L. Blanchard, rebuking the immodesty of a burlesque of the 'eighties, concluded his notice with the witty remark: "The Misses (giving their names) played the nobles of the court, and, it must be confessed, allowed very little to come betwixt the wind and their nobility." The Living Pictures at the Palace in 1895 evoked a remonstrance from Mr Coote, the secretary of the National Vigilance Association, who with the morbid sensitiveness to sexual impressions which characterizes the self-appointed guardians of public morals, pronounced them "the ideal form of indecency, shameful productions, deserving the condemnation of all right-thinking people." It is interesting that with the passing of burlesque nudity became æstheticized in the Poses Plastiques and Tableaux Vivants which were a feature of the new Theatres of Variety, then superseding and 'elevating' the old-time Music Hall. In this respect musical comedy, the natural successor of burlesque, preserved an absolute decorum. George Edwardes, who had begun as D'Oyly Carte's manager, entered into partnership with and then succeeded John Hollingshead at the Gaiety, and was now emperor of this kind of entertainment, discovered, as C. B. Cochran rediscovered in the late nineteen-twenties, that there is as much sex-appeal in clothes as in nudity. He dressed his young ladies instead of undressing them, and musical comedy never scandalized the vigilance committees.

But it was not nudity that killed burlesque. It had already ceased to be an art-form by the end of the 'sixties when it fell into contempt as a *baisser de rideau*. In 1876 it enjoyed a temporary revival at the Gaiety when Hollingshead introduced the three-act burlesque and the famous quartette, but writers of burlesque for the Gaiety started under a heavy disadvantage. Their play of fancy was limited. They were no longer required to be original in treatment of character. What they were expected to do was to provide opportunities for the Gaiety favourites: to invent a comic character for Fred Leslie, a part in which Nellie Farren's vivacity might run riot, and lines for young ladies who could not speak them. And so the Gaiety burlesque became a string of music-hall songs with a bundle of ancient 'wheezes' held weakly together by an attenuated story which lived through Act I and was totally lost in the succeeding acts. It depended not on the author, but on imported variety turns and the individual talents of the performers for gagging, 'business,' and imitation.

The Gaiety principals, however, commanded an army of worshippers in all classes of society. Each lady had her own chosen 'colours.' These were at one time made up in scarves and sold by the St James's hosiers, who traded in old school ties, to adoring mashers who sported them in the stalls like the rival factions of the Byzantine circus.[1] Nor were the gallery boys behind in their fealty to their favourites. The welcome they gave to Nellie Farren and Fred Leslie on their return in 1889, after eighteen months' absence in Australia and the United States, was one of 'revivalist' enthusiasm. Seats were already booked the day they left England's shores. On the opening night four thousand people fought for admission to the theatre, which held only 1250.

This Indian summer of burlesque was only of brief duration. With the sudden and tragic death of Leslie at the age of thirty-seven and the retirement of Nellie Farren, crippled by the habit of sprinkling water on her fleshings so that no crinkle in the gleaming silk should show across the footlights, the "sacred lamp" was finally extinguished. Her successors wore long dresses covering the ankles. "The Gaiety Girl"—the first of a long series of Girl titles—introduced a new form of "musical variety farce" which soon became a formidable rival to the music hall and attracted those of its patrons who objected to the convention which obliged them to drink during the whole of the performance and sit in a fog of tobacco smoke. Also in 1889 the imitations and topical parodies which had been a salient feature of latter-day burlesque found a new medium in the Revue, a form of entertainment borrowed, as its name implies, from France. The first full-programme English Revue, *Potpourri*, set a pattern to which its descendants have, on the whole, adhered. It consisted mainly of a liberal chaffing of eminent men and women of the stage, skits on plays of the hour, and "the kind of fun that is found

---

[1] It was not only the male sex that indulged in this foolish adulation of stage favourites. The first feminine fan club, as it would now be termed, was formed in the 'nineties by the admirers of Lewis Waller. They stood for hours in queues to see him enter or leave the theatre, and called themselves "The Keen Order of Wallerites," a title which was soon abbreviated with Cockney humour into "The KOWS."

at a fashionable supper party." It drew fresh talent from the halls, including one of the cleverest of mimics, Marie Dainton. The *genre* originated with a short revue as part of a triple bill at the Court in 1893. *Under the Clock* was written by Charles Brookfield and Seymour Hicks. It made fun of Sherlock Holmes and contained a skit *The Third Mrs Tanqueray*.

On December 16, 1897, death, which had untimely taken the last genius of burlesque, claimed the last hero of old-time melodrama. A madman struck down William Terriss as he went into the stage-door of the Adelphi. His murder marked the passing of the kind of melodrama so long associated with the theatre where he died. The old transpontine and Adelphi melodrama was written for the pit and gallery; it was a drama composed of sensational incidents and violent appeals to the emotions. In those days the terms drama and melodrama were almost synonymous. There is a story of a young author approaching Barry Sullivan with a play. "I have written a drama," he began, but was cut short by Sullivan, who announced majestically: "I never act in drama. I am a tragedian."

The word melodrama has so come down in the world by dint of loose and derogatory usage that it is not amiss to remark that it is, as farce is to comedy, the necessary complement to tragedy in its comment on life. The latter are concerned with conduct, the former with circumstance. And, in the words of R. L. Stevenson, "there is a vast deal in life where the interest turns, not upon what a man shall choose to do, but on how he manages to do it; not on the passionate slips and hesitations of the conscience, but on the problems of the body and of the practical intelligence, in clean open-air adventure, the shock of arms or the diplomacy of life." Melodrama, in its right interpretation, is a serious play in which the incidents control and determine conduct. Actions speak louder than character; to do is more important than to be. The characters of the early melodramas were not drawn with any subtlety. They were broadly conceived, being simply good or bad, partly because, as G. K. Chesterton pointed out, "the essence of melodrama is that it appeals to the moral sense in a highly simplified form, the object of the simplification being to gain a resounding rapidity of action which subtlety would obstruct"; and partly because this simplification of the characters makes it easier for the spectator to put himself in their place and to imagine that what is happening to them is happening to him. The destiny which governs Hamlet weighs also on the head of the uncomplex heroes of melodrama, but it is—or was—easier for the spectator to identify himself with these noble simpletons than with the Prince of Denmark. Thirdly, the mood of undaunted optimism that prevails in melodrama satisfies those who find illusion in the theatre, for its world is a just and lucky world in which things fall out fitly, in which poetic justice never fails to operate, in which the virtuous lead charmed lives, and vice is disposed of by a comfortable providence.

During the second half of the nineteenth century melodrama was gradually changing. In the 'fifties the only development was in mechanical ingenuity, in the contrivance of sensational feats of scene-shifting and stage carpentry, in those optical illusions used in spook plays, like *The Corsican Brothers*, Dion Boucicault's horror play *The Vampire*, and *Selfishness* (City of London Theatre, 1856), a most original play for its time in which the hero's conscience appeared as an accompanying wraith. As train smashes, shipwrecks, and collapsing bridges lost their originality, there followed a vogue for additional gymnastics, introduced by Dion Boucicault in *The Colleen Bawn* in 1860. The actors were called upon for a display of acrobatics, having to scale ivy-covered towers or leap from precipices, until as melodrama came to rely almost entirely on tricks of plot and stage effect its characters became more and more preposterous, its action more and more unintelligible, and its dialogue more and more commonplace and even ungrammatical. It was already ripe for parody in 1864, when Tom Taylor burlesqued it in *Sense and Sensation*.

The failure of the revival of *Peep o' Day*, one of the most popular melodramas of the 'fifties, which ran originally for a year, called forth a critical stricture on the deterioration of public taste. "Modern audiences seek for incident alone and are as a rule intolerant of anything that delays or suspends the action." As the popularity of this kind of hectic melodrama waned, it became distinguished by the derogatory epithet 'transpontine'—a withering adjective in the 'eighties—because of the particular favour it enjoyed in the theatres on the South side of the Thames.

An important landmark in the development of melodrama was Henry Arthur Jones's *The Silver King*, produced by Wilson Barrett in 1882. "I should never have written melodrama," Jones afterwards stated, "if Wilson Barrett had not been the only manager who would look at my work in the early days. But I am glad I did learn to write it because a knowledge of melodrama gives a sinewy and vertebrate frame to the work of a young dramatist and chastens him from the vice of substituting his own 'ideas' for a plot." *The Silver King* was enormously successful. In 1925 Jones's publishers stated that the play had been performed every week-night somewhere ever since its first production. It freed the author to write the kind of plays he wanted to, and it provoked the praise of no less a person than Matthew Arnold, the Messiah of Culture, who pronounced it to be literature. What was new in *The Silver King* was that the inner drama of the hero, who mistakenly believes that he is guilty of murder, takes precedence over the outer drama of coincidence. In fact, the train-smash, which is a pivotal incident in the story and would have been a sensational feature of the old transpontine melodrama, is only narrated to the audience.

"There is nothing transpontine," said Matthew Arnold, "in *The Silver King*. In general in drama of this kind the diction and sentiments, like the incidents, are extravagant, impossible, transpontine; here they are not. Throughout the piece the diction and sentiments are natural, they have sobriety and propriety, they are literature. It is an excellent and hopeful sign to find playwrights capable of writing in this style, a public capable of enjoying it."

Some credit must be given to Dion Boucicault for the improvement of melodrama. His Irish melodramas, *The Colleen Bawn* (which enjoyed a run of 230 performances in 1860), *Arra-na-Pogue*, and *The Shaugraun* show a marked advance in characterization and especially in dialogue. "Didn't I lave the world to follow ye?" replies Myles-na-Coppaleen when Eily O'Connor asks him if he still loves her. "And since then there's bin neither night nor day in my life. I lay down on Glenna Point above where I see this cottage, and I live in the sight of it. Oh, Eily, if tears were pison to the grass, there wouldn't be a fresh blade on Glenna Hill this day." And this is the admonition of the hero to his favoured rival as he joins his hand to that of the woman he loves: "When ye cease to love her may dyin' become ye; and when ye do die, lave your money to the poor, your widdy to me, and we'll both forgive ye." His dialogue sometimes has the musical rhythm and native poetry which is the Irishman's natural endowment. There is freshness, wit, pathos, and rough humour as well as carpentry in Dion Boucicault's plays. His dialogue is a break with the conventional turgid rhetoric which lingers even in

The Silver King. But Jones's diction, though in the old tradition, did not, according to Arnold, "overstep the modesty of nature." Denver's famous apostrophe when he believes that he has committed murder: "O God, roll back Thy universe and give me yesterday!" was, as William Archer commented, "not a realistic remark, but a natural thought vigorously expressed."

Boucicault was also a pioneer in subtlety of characterization, the next forward step in the progress of melodrama from the transpontine to the 'strong' or romantic play. Conn, the ne'er-do-well of the title and the real hero of *The Shaugraun* (1875)—for he is only the servant of the technical hero and would conventionally have provided only the comic relief—is a marked advance in individualization on any previous melodrama character. As long as audiences remained naïve and melodrama was written for the lower levels of intelligence, type-characterization was sufficient. It is easier to follow as well as less difficult to write. And at first, as the intellectual level of the public rose, individualization was less the work of the playwright than of the actor. Irving had early shown his talent for this when in 1868 he acted the part of Bill Sikes in John Oxenford's dramatization of *Oliver Twist.* E. R. Russell wrote of this performance: "In the grim brutality of Sikes's face as realized by Mr Irving there lives an awful brooding, a rooted bitterness of loathing for himself, his life, his luck, his surroundings." In the callous, unmitigated ruffian of Dickens's conception there is no hint at all of this, even in the novel.

The individualization of Mathias in *The Bells*, the realization of the double parts in *The Lyons Mail* and *The Corsican Brothers*, were superimposed by Irving on the sketchily drawn type-creations of their authors. These were in a real sense creations of the actor and he was constantly enlarging them. As Dubosc, after cold-bloodedly killing the guard of the Lyons Mail, he used to emphasize his callousness when turning over the body in search of papers by humming a few bars of the *Marseillaise*. One night, seized with a fit of fantastic humour, he substituted *Nearer, My God, to Thee*. Bernard Shaw once wrote: "A really good Adelphi melodrama is of first-rate literary importance because it only needs elaboration to become a masterpiece." He was thinking of elaboration by the playwright, but Irving showed that the vital qualities of imagination, humour, and sense of character could also be supplied by the actor. A striking instance of the way in which the personal aura of the actor's keen imagination can 'inform' (in the Aristotelian sense) the conception of the author was Martin Harvey's gradual creation of Raresby the Rat, the scallywag soldier of fortune in *The Breed of the Treshams*. He has himself told how, after procuring an exact reproduction of a pair of seventeenth-century cavalier boots, a real buff coat with a proper rider's flare to the skirts and a plumed hat worn back to front to give its feathers a rakish angle, he underwent "the curious psychological experience of a romantic abstraction fretting to come to life." With every added touch, a new attitude or bit of business—the short clay pipe, the Hollywood moustache, the rakishly cocked sword, the bestriding of a chair or sitting on a table with one foot on a chair, the fighting of the duel without removing the pipe from his mouth—the insolent, devil-may-care cavalier took possession of him, even to the extent of dispossessing the actor's natural dreamy, meek, and moth-like self, so that he found it "a psychological and physical impossibility to moderate his reading of the character." So much was it a creation of the actor's that the two ladies who had written the play were horrified when they saw it. They accused him of prostituting their work and threatened to forbid its performance.

With the disappearance of the old-style tragedian the romantic actor, who succeeded him, favoured the "strong" drama. This differed from the old melodrama (a title the new actor-manager objected to) in that it was built round a central character—which gave him an opportunity for the kind of subtly thought-out creation we have just been speaking about, and instead of being merely a concatenation of incidents frittering away the interest of the story—what Dick Swiveller would have called "an accumulation of staggerers"—it "imagined one bizarre and wildly improbable situation and then devoted infinite pains to the adjustment of the springs, levers, and cogwheels of an elaborate and lifeless mechanism for leading up to one startling tableau." This was Archer's analysis of the Victorian Sardou formula. The central figure ceased to be the hero, in the old Adelphi acceptance of the term, for his very essence was unsubtlety. All that had been required of him was a gallant breeziness, an indomitable and uncompromising virility. It was said of William Terriss, the most adored of all Adelphi heroes—infatuated ladies sent him jewellery and servant girls waited at the stage door to hand him posies—that he was "so frank that he was unable to suggest intrigue of any kind; his strength was in a bold and forceful honesty." The romantic actor's strength was subtlety, pathos, and ironic humour. And together with the change in the hero-type the moral values of melodrama changed. Poetic justice no longer operated unexceptionally. Even the tradition of the happy ending was violated. The hero was humanized by the addition of human weaknesses. He became the drunken wastrel of *The Only Way*, rewarded for his noble self-sacrifices—"It is a far, far better thing I do than I have ever done," he said on the steps of the guillotine—not with the hand of the heroine, but with the "far, far better rest I go to than I have ever known." Or else the villain was allowed to steal his thunder and the limelight was focused on Baron Scarpia or on the jovially sinister Chief of the Russian Secret Police in *The Red Lamp*, one of Beerbohm Tree's richest melodramatic creations. Similarly the adventuress was raised in the social scale, painted in natural colours, and made more interesting than the heroine.

In 1896 Clement Scott, like a duenna of Victorian morality, protested against "the new system of white-washing villains in order to avoid conventionality," and piously ejaculated: "It will be a bad day for drama when the clear note of justice is sounded no more." "How cynical the stage is growing," exclaimed another critic, commenting on a play in which there was "only one loyal, manly man, and he a bit of a cad, and only one good pure woman, and she a bit of a fool." Oscar Wilde had written in the *Dramatic Review* (May 30, 1885): "Perfect heroes are the monsters of melodrama and have no place in dramatic art. Life possibly contains them, but Parnassus often rejects what Peckham may welcome. I look forward to a reaction in favour of the cultured criminal." That also was to come. It still wanted two decades before sympathy was invited for the first criminal hero in 'Raffles' and still longer before the villain actually became the hero in *Mr Wu* and *The Green Goddess*. Over a century earlier Dr Johnson had observed *à propos* poetic justice:

> Whatever pleasure there may be in seeing crimes punished and virtue rewarded, yet, since wickedness often prospers in real life, the poet is certainly at liberty to give it prosperity on the stage. For if poetry is an imitation of reality, how are its laws broken by exhibiting the world in its true form? The stage may sometimes gratify our wishes, but if it be truly "the mirror of life" it ought to show us sometimes what we are to expect.

In 1896, however, if not in 1895, the playgoing public showed that it did not want the stage to be truly the mirror of life. The intellectual theatre had fought the first round of its modern battle against the theatre of comfortable illusion and lost it. The playwright or the manager who sought to impose upon the public Cromwell's rule—not what they like, but what is good for them—found himself up against the self-satisfied, after-dinner stupidity of the stalls (Pinero once suggested that they should have high tea before going to the theatre), and a growing spirit of derision in the gallery. Jones's *The Triumph of the Philistines* (1895) was mercilessly booed on the first night and ran for only forty performances. The hostile reception the following year of his *Michael and His Lost Angel* damped the courage of the most earnest dramatist of the time, for his only rival, Pinero, was merely playing the new game according to the safe, old rules. G.B.S., infuriated by the critical snobbery which hailed *The Notorious Mrs Ebbsmith* as a masterpiece, wrote of him: "He conquered the public by the exquisite flattery of giving them plays they really liked while pretending that such appreciation is only possible from persons of great culture and intellectual acuteness."

The 'nineties were a difficult time for managers. Old Squire Bancroft had retired in 1888, confessing to only four failures and a net profit of £180,000 in twenty years of management. Walking through the West End, where fifteen new theatres had been opened since he first started there, from his flat in the Albany to lunch at the Garrick or dine at the Athenæum, a familiar figure with his mass of white hair crowned by a broad flat-brimmed silk hat and a black-rimmed eye-glass on a black ribbon of watered silk, he must have smiled to himself to see so much chopping and changing. In their uncertainty as to which way the cat was going to jump, every London management rejected

Edward Rose's dramatization of *The Prisoner of Zenda* in 1895. Yet romantic melodrama was to be the vogue for the next ten years. Only after the production of *The Prisoner of Zenda*, by Edward Sothern, in New York, did George Alexander take the risk. With it in 1896 he stopped a rot at the St James's, and it earned him a net profit of £50,000.

Were the romantic melodramas and the light comedies which monopolized the theatre in the last years of the century a proof of the eternal sentimental eagerness of the British public to escape from the realities of life, of its ineradicable taste for the showy and meretricious? Or were they accepted *faute de mieux* because the new playwrights had not acquired the new technique, because the new plays still wore the fashions of yesterday; because, as Shaw explained it, "the modern manager must not produce *The Wild Duck*, but he must be very careful not to produce a play which will seem insipid and old-fashioned to playgoers who may have seen *The Wild Duck* even though they may have hissed it." It is difficult to believe that Ibsenism had as yet so far unsettled theatre-goers. It is true that *John Gabriel Borkman* reached the London stage only four months after its Scandinavian première in 1887, but it attracted only the ardent Ibsenites. And Tree's experiment with *The Master Builder* was not encouraging. The success of *The Prisoner of Zenda* had set the tune. The managers who had refused the play were quick to learn their lesson. There was a veritable tarara-boom-de-ay of twopence-coloured, Ruritanian romance, and swashbucklery, which would have delighted the heart of Robert Louis Stevenson.

It must have been a very small section of the general playgoing public which had become impatient of the old-fashioned play, judging by the success of *A Man's Shadow* at Her Majesty's in 1897. This was an old-fashioned melodrama, if ever there was one. It was a translation from the French, with all the familiar ingredients, a theatrically effective double hero-villain part, a sensational courtroom scene, and a comic underplot. Reviewing it, William Archer wrote: "The pit and the gallery loved it, and nowadays, as we see on all hands, the stalls, half cynically, half obsequiously, take their cue from the pit." The plot of the play is based on the absurd altruism of the hero as much as on his unfortunate physical resemblance to a scoundrel. Wrongly accused because of this resemblance, he allows himself to be convicted of robbery and murder, and sent as a convict to Devil's Island, leaving his wife and little daughter to the charity of an old servant. Why? So that his friend may not discover that the woman he has married is unworthy. Even when his friend has died after learning the facts from another source, he still refuses to clear himself. Having suffered first to save his friend's happiness, he now sacrifices himself to save the reputation of his friend's memory.

The willing acceptance of absurdities in the old trans-pontine melodrama written for the lower classes has been interpreted as revealing an idealizing instinct in the masses which people of culture often lack. But the audiences at Her Majesty's were cultured audiences. They were the kind of audience among whom four years before H. A. Jones had noted "a growing dissatisfaction with the old stale devices of the theatre and a growing disposition to welcome a less childish and trivial form of English drama." They were the kind of audience of whom Shaw had written in 1895 that they were "getting tired of the old-fashioned plays faster than actors were learning to make the new ones effective." In his vituperation of the "monotony and vulgarity of drama in which passion is everything and intellect nothing" he spoke apparently for a very small minority.

The vast majority of the playgoers of the 'nineties still went to the theatre, as their fathers had done, to feel and not to think. To Shaw himself, on his own admission, there was no illusion in the theatre; for him the play was not the thing, but its thought, its purpose, its feeling, and its execution. To the playgoers of the 'nineties, even to Archer, the theatre was "the place of light and sound, of mystery and magic." They were indifferent to the drama's thought and purpose. And so far the old school of criticism was justified in its defence of the more popular forms of drama; in their belief that the theatre should "follow the indications of success instead of isolating itself from the public of whose feelings it should be the living expression." The public could be led and educated, as was to be proved, to appreciate a drama with a moral value and ideal, but the time was not yet. It could get used to everything, even to being insulted, and enjoy it into the bargain. And in 1898 Shaw, who had begun the work of education by scarifying romanticism in the columns of the *Saturday Review*, boldly took the financial risk of publishing his *Plays Pleasant and Unpleasant* as the only adequate means of reaching the public they were designed to interest.

As the century drew to a close the play was not the thing. The attraction of the theatre was the performer, as it nearly always is. What a potent influence 'star value' and 'box-office names' have become in the modern theatre! The 'nineties were the high summer of the actor and the actress. How seldom did the author's name appear in lights! People went to the theatre, not because of the dramatist, but to see Irving and Ellen Terry, Charles Wyndham and Mary Moore, Cyril Maude and Winifred Emery; not to hear *Hamlet*, but to see Forbes Robertson. They swallowed romantic fustian for the sake of Fred Terry and Julia Neilson or of Lewis Waller. They were lured to Maeterlinck, not by the reputation of "the Belgian Shakespeare," but by the fact that Mrs Patrick Campbell was appearing as Mélisande. They even suffered poetry for the sake of Tree and Alexander. So strong was the position of the actor-manager that when in 1897 Forbes Robertson appeared in a horribly vulgar travesty of history, called *Nelson's Enchantress*, the actor-manager rebuked the audience from the stage for its demonstration of disapproval. A critic noted on this occasion: "Instead of indignant audiences throwing things on the stage as in the bad old days, we shall soon see managing actors and actors pelting the people for daring to have an opinion of their own." And when Clement Scott delivered himself of an indiscreet utterance about the morality of the stage, implying that no girl could become an actress and remain an honest woman—a charge there is no reason to think more justified than at any other period—a combined protest by the leading West End actor-managers to the editor of the *Daily Telegraph* resulted in the dismissal of the old war-horse of Victorian traditions. And so with the passing of the century passed the leader of the Old Guard of dramatic criticism.

VI

A NEW HORIZON

The Nineteen Hundreds

THE turn of the century and the disappearance of the leader of the Ancients began a period of militant criticism. The battle for an intellectual theatre was not to be timorously abandoned because of the temporary defeat. The public was going to be given what was good for it whether it wanted it or no. The all-powerful actor-manager bore the brunt of the attack, for it was he who was giving or doing his best to give the public what it wanted; trying if possible to secure for himself a fortune by an astute flattery of its prejudices and susceptibilities, pandering to its distaste for realism and its naïve delight in the romantic and the spectacular, confining his æsthetic enthusiasms to the scenic illustration of his plays and the physical comfort of his audiences.

The actor-managers could afford to ignore the critical assumption that because the plays they put on were devoid of merit they must therefore be rejecting meritorious plays by unacted authors. The charge that the actor-manager discouraged new dramatists was hardly true even of Irving, whose "Damn the English drama" was to be for ever held against him. A number of untried playwrights had their chance. Haddon Chambers, H. V. Esmond, and Captain Marshall made their names. That they happened to be disciples of Robertson rather than of Ibsen, however much it disappointed the prophets of a "thinking theatre," could hardly be held against the actor-managers as long as the public paid to see their plays. It is true that Irving turned down *The Man of Destiny* when submitted to him by G. B. Shaw, but it is not surprising that the actor was not favourably inclined towards an author who instructed him in quite uncustomarily voluminous stage-directions exactly how to act the part he had written for him. On the other hand, Irving gave very practical encouragement to the young J. M. Barrie; "drove him," so Barrie declared, to write his first three plays and helped him to find a manager to produce them. Barrie, of course, was already a very successful novelist whereas Shaw's attempts at the novel had been failures, and his unorthodox conception of a play was bewildering to actors and managers alike. Nevertheless, Cyril Maude commissioned a play from Shaw, but the resultant *You Never can Tell*, when put into rehearsal, so flummoxed the actors that two of the leading members of the cast walked out, and Herbert Trench, Maude's partner in the management of the Haymarket, insisted on the project being abandoned.

Barrie did not at first fall completely under the spell of the theatre. His approach to playwriting, as he himself has confessed, was "rather contemptuous." This was the attitude of most men of letters at the end of the nineteenth century and probably, in part at any rate, accounts for their failure in it. Barrie was saved by a rare instinctive craftsmanship even when he was only "trifling with the stage." When he began to take it seriously the result was truly astonishing. *The Wedding Guest*, his first serious play, produced at the Garrick on September 27, 1900, was of all things a problem play; a play which faced facts, the thing most alien to Barrie's nature and the thing the public had shown itself most reluctant to do in the theatre. It looks as though Barrie had let himself be convinced by the propaganda for the thinking theatre that the future lay with it. The play at all events persuaded Archer that he was a new recruit to Ibsenism. Unfortunately he chose a moral issue which must have been growing a little stale by 1900. An artist, noble at heart, and truly repentant of a solitary wild oat, is confronted on the day of his marriage to sweet innocence by his ex-mistress, who arrives with his infant child. It was the subject Pinero had dealt with twelve years previously in *The Profligate*. The otherwise irreproachable husband faced with the one slip of his past, the naïvely idealizing wife, and the Painted Lady, who is not as bad as she is painted, belong to Oscar Wilde's stock-in-trade. Was Barrie imitatively trying to step into their shoes or did he mean to preach a sermon on the growing laxness of morality, to point the deplorable outcome of the defiance of convention? One might perhaps think this. "To know that you loved me was enough," cries the erring woman in explanation of her sin. "I was willing to let all else go. I was up to date. Up to date!"

In 1903 another novelist turned playwright. Somerset Maugham was then the author of four published but not remunerative novels. In view of his admitted purpose to win financial independence by his writing it is interesting to find that his maiden play *A Man of Honour* was also a fact-facing, realistic, problem play. He wrote it, no doubt, not as Barrie had apparently written *The Wedding Guest*, as a rather uncongenial endeavour to qualify as a serious dramatist, but because the creative artist in him prompted him to write of people and things he knew about. At that date this was a mistake for a playwright who hoped to make money out of the theatre, more especially as the people his experience as a medical student in St Thomas's Hospital had made him familiar with were the Cockney poor. The complacent middle-class theatre-goer was not yet interested in the lower orders as represented on the stage; they preferred the antics of the contemptible "smart set" as amusingly satirized by Alfred Sutro in *The Walls of Jericho*, in which—such was the change in the moral outlook—the only virtuous character was an elderly lady, who after a career that included "a little accident" had married a wealthy peer. *A Man of Honour* dealt with the problem of the marriage of a man and a woman of different social levels: the theme, in fact, of *Caste*, a play which had not yet outlived its popularity, doubtless because of Robertson's essentially false, idealistic treatment. Maugham made the mistake, financially speaking, of treating it honestly and realistically, and he was quick to realize it. Admittedly, there was this difference in the theme: the union of Basil Kent (played by a young and coming actor, Harley Granville Barker) and Jenny Bush was not founded on love. The cultured and educated solicitor had drifted into an affair with the Cockney barmaid, and only his conventional sense of honour, his acceptance of the code which required a seducer to make an honest woman of his victim, had made him marry her when it appeared that she was pregnant. However true to life, this honest picture of the degrading matrimonial squabbles of the ill-assorted pair, ending in Jenny's suicide, had no hope of finding favour on the commercial stage of 1903. But it was grist to the mill of that "assiduous but joyless institution," the Stage Society, which, fighting for a natural, thinking theatre, gave it a matinée production. Like Jenny Bush's baby, it barely survived its birth. It was written too soon. It illustrated a personal conviction, not generally shared, that the lower classes were perfectly contented as they were and had no desire to live as their betters lived, and an idea which was only beginning to gain ground that a great deal of human unhappiness was caused by false idealism and the irrational acceptance of moral standards that custom had imposed. We have to wait another nine years before the stage could dare—in Stanley Houghton's *Hindle Wakes* and Galsworthy's *The Eldest Son*—defy the convention which demanded that a fallen girl should be redeemed by a loveless marriage with the man who had seduced her.

Maugham at once drew the conclusions of his failure. His practical aim of independence decided him to write to the tastes of the public. He was later to outdo *The Walls of Jericho* in *Our Betters*. But in the meanwhile, before he began the series of light, satiric comedies, built out of the stock subjects of the successful dramatist, which brought him the success he coveted, he carefully considered the requirements of the public. In *Andalusia: Sketches and Impressions*, written in 1905, two years before his second play *Lady Frederick*, he made this reflection:

> We English are idealists; and on the stage especially reality stinks in our nostrils. The poor are vulgar, and in our franker moments we confess our wish to have nothing to do with them. The middle classes are sordid; we have enough of them in real life, and no desire to observe their doings in the theatre, particularly when we wear our evening clothes. But when a dramatist presents duchesses to our admiring eyes, we feel in our element; we watch the acts of persons whom we would willingly meet at dinner, and our craving for the ideal is satisfied.

So for a while he added his contribution to the store of amusing plays with well-bred and titled persons, their marital infidelities, triangular love affairs, and social ambitions; spiced them with epigrams in the manner of Oscar Wilde, and soon had three plays running concurrently.

Maugham's assessment of the English taste may be

assumed to be pretty accurate. Tree reflected the prevalent taste when he remarked: "A work of art should make us say 'Ah!'—not 'Ugh!'" The trouble with Ibsen had been that he provoked too may 'Ughs' at a time when both 'Ughs' and 'Ahs' came much more readily to expression than to-day. The trouble with the Stage Society and the other dilettante societies of the 'nineties which were trying to slap the intellectual drama into life was that they were more fascinated by an 'ugh-play' than by an 'ah-play.' But at the turn of the century the worship of Ibsen had begun to go out of fashion. In 1902 the *Daily Telegraph* noted: "It is a curious and, in a sense, significant fact that Ibsen's works have of late completely disappeared from the stage. The cult, it is true, was never a very widespread one, but having regard to the intensity displayed some years ago by its supporters, one cannot but feel surprise at the brief duration of their enthusiasm." The reason was that the votaries of the new theatre had switched their devotion to Bernard Shaw. He had been taken up by the Stage Society, with a membership of about 400 and a limited revenue of some £1500. His plays, now published, began to be talked about—though, if we except a pirated version of *Cashel Byron's Profession*, in which the famous prize-fighter, Gentleman Jim Corbett, credited with the ambition to play Hamlet, was touring the United States in the title rôle—they had so far earned no money. The Germans, as always eager to assert their cultural superiority over the Philistine British, were adopting him, as they had adopted Shakespeare and Wilde, as part of their intellectual and artistic *Lebensraum*, but the great British Public, whose prejudices he flouted as indifferently as he flouted all theatrical prudence, remained apathetic.

Two things combined to win for Shaw belated recognition at home. The first was the devout enthusiasm of one disciple, the young actor-dramatist Harley Granville Barker, who had been actively associated with the Stage Society productions. The second was the seemingly uncorrelated fact that it had been the habit of the well-to-do in the 'eighties and the 'nineties to have large families. Shaw's sudden vogue, which Archer described as "an outburst of latent or suppressed popularity," began with the Vedrenne-Barker Court Theatre venture at the end of the year 1903. Vedrenne in his anxiety to secure the services of Barker as producer was persuaded to agree to the latter's stipulation that he should be allowed to put on a series of Shaw's plays. The Vedrenne-Barker association was not a repertory theatre. It was really an extension of the Stage Society policy, in which new plays, instead of being put on for a single matinée, as they were by the Stage Society, were given a run of three matinées a week for two weeks. Afternoon performances were less a matter of choice than of necessity, for only so was it possible to cast them with West End actors and actresses who were otherwise engaged in the evenings. This proved a happy accident because the matinées attracted a quite different type of audience. It excluded the tired business-man, for whom in the main the commercial theatre was run and who had no time to waste in the afternoon. Such males as frequented them were either literary or theatrical, and thanks to the assiduous canvassing of the Sidney Webbs and Shaw's worldly-wise insistence that *John Bull's Other Island* should be held over till the House was sitting there was a fair sprinkling of politicians. But the audiences were preponderantly feminine and even these were not the regular theatre-goers. F. C. Burnand thus analysed a Shaw audience at the Court: "The female element prodominates over the inferior sex as something like twelve to one. The audience had not a theatre-going, but rather a lecture-going, sermon-loving appearance. It was difficult to tire them out, but they did become wearied."

There were no matinée idols at the Court. These ladies went to it for the sake of the play. Who were these earnest, enduring women who preferred a play like *Major Barbara*, frankly labelled "a discussion," to the choice of H. B. Irving's or Martin Harvey's *Hamlet* or J. M. Barrie's *Alice Sit-by-the-Fire* with Ellen Terry? They were girls like those in Mr Barrie's play: young ladies who "always went to the thinking theatre." They were the grown-up daughters of business and professional men, born at the time when large families were the rule. The elder were now of marriageable age, having been educated for the sole end of matrimony by a succession of French and German governesses and such foreign travel as consisted in accompanying their parents to the fashionable watering-places of the Continent at the proper season. They could paint in water-colours or do hand-embroidery, sing drawing-room ballads, or give a creditable rendering of Chaminade on the piano. They could make polite conversation, perform genteelly on the tennis court with the impediment of long skirts and petti-coats, and waltz more or less divinely. Such were con-sidered by their parents to be the requisite accomplish-ments for wedlock, and no parents doubted that in due course, with the assistance of a skilful maternal strategy, some eligible bachelor would appear, able and eager to support their daughter in the luxury to which she had been accustomed. But, quite apart from the fact that there were not enough eligible bachelors to go round, this generation of girls had different ideas. Many were not enchanted with the prospect of a life-long continuance, be it with a husband, or, failing one, at home, of the routine of social duties and the pursuit of trivial pleasure. Without being rebellious, much less militant, they were New Women. They felt the frustration of the narrowness of domesticity. Women were doing things they had never done before. In the last decade of Queen Victoria's reign the proportion of female clerks had grown from eight to eighteen in every hundred. In 1902 there were already three women teachers to every male. Women yearned for the greater freedom the suffragettes proclaimed as woman's right. Girls who had no necessity to earn their own living began to envy those who did. Feminism, although its political manifestations were still generally regarded as a distasteful aberration, was breeding a new individuality. In a world of changing values and ideas girls were discovering how much there was to learn. The cult of self-perfection was replaced by the ambition to do something worth while. Cheap manuals and extension lectures on science, philosophy, and politics, intended for a new self-educating class, opened their eyes to the shortcomings of their general education. Their younger sisters were already going to boarding schools, which were now coming into fashion, learning subjects of which their own governesses had been ignorant, reading books without parental censorship. They had seen the discontinuance of the custom of family prayers after confessing through childhood in chorus with the servants to the leather-upholstered back of a dining-room chair that they were miserable sinners. The family still dressed in its Sunday best and went to church on Sundays, but the church parade now seemed as important as the service, and they perhaps suspected that the religion they had unquestioningly accepted was practised by their elders less from conviction than as an example to the lower classes. And so they began to think for themselves; they sermon-tasted, went to lectures, and read books on New Thought and Mind over Matter.

In a word, there was growing up in an age when self-education was at a premium a generation of young women who had nothing much to do except occupy their minds. They found themselves full of bottled-up enthusiasms only seeking a seemingly worthy and exciting object. They were just the audience that Shaw, who used the stage as a pulpit-rostrum, needed. His startling way of saying outspokenly the kind of things they hardly dared to think was just what they wanted to complete their emancipation. And so it was not the grudging appreciation of the critics which gave Shaw his popularity—they, like the Bourbons, had for the most part learnt nothing and forgotten nothing and even when he had attained a world-wide reputation continued to berate him with a condescending irritation for not writing the kind of play they thought he ought to write—but rather his first impact on young and lively minds. A young Chinese amusingly summed up his own impressions in a privately printed booklet, recording "my experience of the man": "When he first came upon me I was simply head over heels mad about him. It was forsooth love at first sight." Forty years later we have seen the power of teen-age hysteria to foist an entertainer to the dizziest heights of popularity. Allowance made for the very different conditions, the influence of juvenile enthusiasm for Shaw must not be underrated. His worshippers took his works with a seriousness that might have been galling to him, had he not been himself to blame. They prated of what they (and he) called the Shavian philosophy until, intrigued, inveigled or coerced, the elder generation finally bought seats when Shaw was at last accorded the long-denied recognition of evening performance at a West End theatre.

The success of the Vedrenne-Barker seasons was mainly due to Shaw, but they also brought into the theatre three men of literary distinction: Galsworthy, Laurence Housman, and St John Hankin. With Granville Barker himself, these formed the nucleus of an intellectual drama. There was only one thing wrong with the Court venture. It did not pay. It was immensely praised. Cultured people talked about it, wrote about it, discussed it. Banquets were given in its honour. But, with the peculiarity of cultured audiences, very few bought seats. It justified the belief that there was a minority that wanted thinking plays, but it also proved that this minority was not sufficiently large to support it. In a note to J. E. Vedrenne, dated May 16, 1906, when evening performances had been introduced at the Court, G.B.S. wrote:

> The average house for matinées was £149 15s. 9d. The average house in the evening up to the end of last week was £92 7s. 6d. Say £85 for the management, £6 18s. od. for the author, and £23 11s. 6d. for the leading lady (Ellen Terry). Net result probably about £2 10s. od. apiece for V and B to live on and pile up future capital for the new theatre. All your real successes (*John Bull* and *Superman*) have been with modest youthful casts.

This was the insoluble problem. The public, as always, wanted box-office names, and box-office salaries ate up the meagre profits. And at the same time new talent was hard to find, for all that the profession was more overcrowded than it had ever been. The trouble was that there was no school for actors. F. R. Benson was achieving in a modest way what had once been the aim of the stock companies, but the provincial theatres were now served by the touring companies sent out by the actor-managers, and the actors in these were trained to mimic the actions of their chiefs with accuracy and submission. At the same time, many of the provincial theatres were being converted into theatres of variety. The intelligent minority in the provinces were tiring of the general mediocrity of these road companies; the less fastidious majority were enticed away from the theatre by the stellar attractions and greater comfort of a newly refined and ambitious music-hall. Furthermore, indoor entertainment suffered from the competition of the recent craze for bicycling and golf.

In London ability and training no longer qualified an actor for an engagement. "An author or manager," wrote John Hare in a letter to *The Times* in 1904, "rarely shows confidence in an actor because he can act a part, but because he can look it." Those who could only act were relegated to the road, where they were condemned to repeat the same performance week after week in imitation of the actor who had created the part in town with scant opportunity to show ability or to learn their job. The few who were fortunate enough to gain a footing on the London stage "disported themselves in a spirit of pure egotism. Instead of working together to produce a single and harmonious result they each claimed their own little pitch and did their best to engross the attention of the spectators. As a result, with few exceptions, actors tended to be over-emphatic while actresses had no other aim than sugary sweetness."

What was the remedy? The Impossibilists, for ever yearning for the unattainable, had switched from Ibsen to a new foible: the endowment of a National Theatre and a Conservatoire. In 1905 a Mr Richard Badger offered a gift of a thousand pounds to the London County Council for the erection of a memorial to Shakespeare. An advisory committee was formed, which suggested the erection of an architectural memorial on a site south of the Thames. There the matter rested until 1908 when a new proposition to put up a statue in Park Crescent roused widespread opposition. S. R. Littlewood, then dramatic critic of the *Chronicle*, organized a meeting at the Lyceum Theatre, with Lord Lylton in the chair, which was attended by all the panjandrums of the theatre. This meeting passed a motion in favour of devoting the money, to which a naturalized German, Karl Meyer, offered to add a further £70,000, to the establishment of a National Theatre as a memorial to the poet. An executive committee was elected, the Shakespeare Memorial Committee was united with the National Theatre Committee, and eventually a site was purchased in South Kensington. Then the war provided an opportune excuse for not proceeding further with the project, for the truth of the matter was that nobody, except the few who had to make a hobby-horse of any visionary panacea for the regeneration of the stage—nobody really wanted a National Theatre.

Miss Horniman, the one person who had unwittingly discovered what the stage needed—repertory—was busy in Dublin sponsoring the Irish poet, W. B. Yeats. The pessimist, as usual, thought the serious theatre doomed. His white hopes had failed him; Jones had retired from the fray and Pinero was not the one to burn his fingers or his boats in the effort to make the public swallow something for which it showed no appetite. That "absurd hybrid, miscalled musical comedy," seemed fast to be driving every other form of drama from the stage. George Edwardes's empire was spreading over the metropolis as the Empires of Messrs Moss and Stoll were spreading over the country. If the taverns of the Strand were thronged with hungry, out-of-work actors whilst chorus girls rattled past in hansoms on their way to the Gaiety stage door and "minor principals" (those supercilious beauties of whom nothing was required but to look ravishing, move gracefully, and sing two lines of an octet) drew £15 a week, the reason was that musical comedy perfectly satisfied the average Englishman's two desires in the theatre: pleasure which cost no effort in the reception and a good laugh. These musical comedies always ran true to pattern; one knew exactly what one was getting. They were built round excellent comedians, and dressed and mounted with a perfection rarely attained on the Continent, from where they were increasingly imported. There was a glamour about the New Gaiety and Daly's which the modern stage has never recaptured. They achieved a genuine romantic cajolery both in and out of the theatre. The emotionally deficient post-war generation failed to discover the secret.

Meanwhile, however little it seemed to progress in any direction, the legitimate theatre was not entirely stagnant. In 1903 Ellen Terry went into management with *The Vikings*. This was an unfamiliar Ibsen, not at all the genuine article, and the production was notable for only the "curious lighting and scenic effects." These were the work of Gordon Craig, whose first opportunity this was to experiment with his ideas of scenic suggestion in place of decoration. He did without the customary footlights, using top-lights instead; not altogether successfully—because the downward shadow cast on the actors' faces by the Vikings' voluminous headgear made facial play ineffective. It was, however, something new, and the word 'atmosphere' crept into the critic's vocabulary. It was a change from the spectacular realism which was still the sole aim of almost every theatrical producer and in which the public delighted. The greater the realism, the more grandiose the spectacle, the better it was pleased. In Tree's production of *The Tempest* the noise of the storm completely drowned the words, but the din of the applause outdid the racket of the storm. There was not wanting voices of protest against this extravagant over-elaboration, particularly in the mounting of Shakespeare's plays. The charge of subordinating poetry to furniture was levelled at Tree, just as in the 'fifties the approbrious epithet 'upholsterer' had been hurled at Charles Kean for the same offence. And when Tree brought a live cow on to the stage in *A Midsummer Night's Dream* the voices rose to a screech of æsthetic horror.

Whether or not Tree's and Kean's method of presenting Shakespeare was an ideal one need not be argued. Certain it is that they both performed an immense service to the stage and to the public by maintaining a high artistic standard according to their lights. In the cafés of Vienna a customer ordering coffee is automatically asked by the waiter: "With or without?"—meaning with or without whipped cream. In the presentation of Shakespeare in England there have always been these two alternatives, the 'with' and the 'without,' the richly upholstered and the plain, ungarnished Shakespeare. The two traditions existed side by side though generally the second was followed less from choice than from necessity. Phelps and F. R. Benson were perforce content to let Shakespeare's poetry supply the deficiencies of scenery; Phelps because lavishness was denied him by the means at his disposal, Benson because he made his offering to the provinces and the exigencies of weekly removal from one town to another made the transportation of elaborate scenery impracticable. The co-existence of the two traditions was an excellent thing. The 'without' school had to make a virtue of necessity, and in Benson's case reliance on elocution and athleticism ("play cricket and like it" was the inexorable rule in Benson's touring company) produced a large proportion of the best actors in the first decade of the century. His training was invaluable at a time when there was no other repertory theatre, and when drawing-room dialogue and Saville Row tailoring were blurring the London actor's articulation and stiffening his joints. But both the 'with' and 'without' schools aimed at realistic presentation. In the eighteen-nineties, however, there had arisen a school of thought which believed that Shakespeare should be presented with no scenic distraction at all. William Poël, like Gordon Craig, had faith in the power of suggestion. An Elizabethan Society was formed, and its production in sixteenth-century conditions was a practical test of the public's capacity to appreciate pure poetry on the stage. They won academic eulogies; the public preferred whipped cream. In an address to the Oxford Union Debating Society on May 28, 1900, Berbohm Tree answered criticisms of his Shakespearean productions by quoting "the brutal but irrefutable logic of figures." In three years, he stated, he had presented at Her Majesty's three plays of Shakespeare —*Julius Cæsar*, *King John*, and *A Midsummer Night's Dream*. Some 240,000 people had seen the first, 170,000 the second, and 220,000 the third. Shakespeare, he concluded, with the proof of his pudding in the eating, "cannot be made toler-able to any large section of the play-going public without the plethora of scenic spectacle and gorgeous costumes which the student regards as superfluous and inappropriate."

The truth was that poetry had ceased to be a public art. This was not in any way disproved by the quite numerous poetic dramas which still continued to be put on, for the young poets who wrote them—Stephen Phillips, Bernard Fagan, Laurance Binyon, and Rudolf Besier—were careful to choose classical and historic themes which provided rich opportunities for splendid picturesqueness. Their poetry, though it served to give a literary cachet to slightly tedious plays and to deceive critics into hailing them as a step for-ward in the history of the drama, was not sufficiently important for the ear to distract the eye. They had learnt from Tennyson's mistakes the lesson that they must be simple and concise. In consequence their imaginative poetry, cramped for elbow-room, demanded no mental effort from their audiences and made no profound impres-sion. Their dramas filled a want because a great many of the leading dramatic actors were old Bensonians who needed some vehicle besides Shakespeare for the display of their special accomplishments: a resonant elocution and the magnificent torsos and calves developed by Benson's athletic training which were as much at ease in costume as they were uncomfortable in modern clothes. The story of Tree's bored listening to Stephen Phillips's reading of his play *Herod* until he came to the stage direction "Trumpets off" indicates how little the poetry mattered as compared to the visual possibilities; his remark when rehearsing *Ulysses* that it was "a very good play to go bankrupt on" points the uncertainty of the popular appeal of the poetic drama. Its production was a feather in the actor-manager's artistic reputation, an answer to the charge of commercialism; and he must be given the credit of knowingly accepting the not inconsiderable risk of losing some of the money earned by less artistic concessions to popular taste. For a time the poetic drama was a costly, glittering toy. It was inevitable that it should degenerate into the resplendent, pseudo-poetic melodrama. *Kismet* and *Chu-Chin-Chow* satisfied equally well the requirements of the declamatory actor and better pleased the public that only wanted to be dazzled. By dispensing with the supererogatory poetry they had the additional merit of earning fortunes. It is interesting to speculate whether Flecker's *Hassan* would have had the same success as *Kismet* if it had been produced in 1911. When it was produced after the war this particular toy had ceased to amuse.

While the fashion lasted, costume melodramas, mostly in line of descent from *Tosca* and period Sardou, were glorified, as David Belasco's Japanese melodrama *The Darling of the Gods* was by Tree, by the same authentic, artistic, and spectacular treatment as he applied to Shakespeare and Stephen Phillips. An erudite historical monograph was supplied gratis with the programme. No pains were spared to persuade the public that they belonged to a higher class of drama. The basic themes of heroism, patriotism, and love were still 'sure-fire,' especially in the suburbs and the provinces, which never grew tired of *The Only Way* and *The Scarlet Pimpernel* as they came round in the big cities as regularly as the Wakes or Quarter Day. They provided a medium for the romantic actor trained in the old Lyceum which came up for auction in 1903, a year before Sir Henry Irving died in harness in the provinces. Their style of acting, more flamboyant and less team spirited than the Bensonian school that was replacing it in London, was in course of disappearing. The last Romantics with their rather makeshift companies were perpetually on the road. They made occasional incursions into the West End, but London audiences, becoming accustomed to a high all-round standard of acting, were impatient of the mediocrity of the lesser members of the cast, that spoilt rather than enhanced the bravura performances of the principals—rich oil portraits as some of them were—splashed with brilliant colour in contrast to the tinted photogravures that were superseding them: H. B. Irving's recreation of his father's famous rôles, Fred Terry's Sir Percy Blakeney, and Martin Harvey's Reresby.

None of these plays had any depth or significance. They were for some curious reason labelled "wholesome" plays as distinct from problem plays, which were considered morbid and unwholesome, or from Bernard Shaw, who was brilliant but unwholesome. C. E. Montague, who as dramatic critic of the *Manchester Guardian* investigated the meaning of this epithet, came to the following conclusion:

> In trying to answer the question one casts an eye over the whole wide firmament of 'wholesome' drama, seeking form or outline in the midst of space, and presently there do come

twinkling into sight, now in one place, now in another, as
the stars do, the only slightly dissimilar stars, at dusk, a mighty
host of variants of one central type of positive character. This
type, in its general lines, is that of the man who is not, as we
say, a bad chap after all; the man who, again, is more wide
awake than he seems; the man who may not have much gift
of the gab, but is sure to come well through a scrimmage;
the man who does not wear his heart on his sleeve, preferring
to wear there a heart much less good than his own, so that
when he turns out an unparalleled brick, the cynical observer
of human nature is knocked all of a heap, the man who,
morally, is a regular lion of generosity, usually crouched, it is
true, but quite prepared to do terrific springs of self-devotion
if the occasion for them be sufficiently fantastic—mentally, too,
a perfect mortar or sunk mine of gumption, with a sluggish
fuse to it, slow to take light, but going off at last in veritable
prodigies of mother-wit and horse sense and other popular
forms of practical wisdom; the man who 'has his faults,'
but still—well, if he drinks he is 'nobody's enemy but his
own,' and at those next-morning hours when a nature
radically bad would be simply ringing for soda-water, he is
delighted to be shot or guillotined for the advantage of comparative strangers; he may not keep appointments, or pay his
tailor, or do his work, and, of course, he is not a 'plaster
saint'; but then he "cannot bear to see a woman cry" and at
any hour of the day or night he is game to adopt a baby, or
soothe death-beds, or renounce, for reasons wildly insubstan-
tial, the satisfaction of the cravings of his honest heart.

Montague then asks the question: Why does the public
wish to revel in the contemplation of this special type—and
suggests that it is perhaps because the type is rather like the
vision that each of us, in his moments of maximum complacency, has of himself. He concludes ironically:

It may quite well be better for digestion, especially after
that hard day in the city, if the mind be gently laid on board a
helmless barque and drifted down luxurious streams of vague,

rather washy complacency, than if it be pulled up, one short hour after dinner, by the very sight and sound of some grim, fierce-fanged truth that we knew to be true but were trying to keepsafely out of our minds, like the irreparableness of all action and the extreme difficulty of squaring God with conduct.

It looked as if the Edwardian habit of dining late and abundantly was relegating to the afternoon theatre the plaguey dramatist who, instead of flattering his audience's self-esteem, insisted on unsettling his ideas. After that "hard day in the city" the average evening playgoer went to the theatre in the childish spirit of Let's Pretend. He was content and eager to be persuaded that what he saw was actual life, and if what he generally saw there bore only a very slight resemblance to actual life the illusion that it did was created as much by his willing collaboration as by the trickery of the dramatist. The first dramatists to give him actual life so naturalistically that there was no need for pretence were John Galsworthy, whose *The Silver Box* had been one of the highlights of the Vedrenne-Barker productions, and Charles McEvoy, whose *David Ballard* sent home its first audience from Miss Horniman's repertory theatre in Manchester feeling like Cortez on a peak in Darien. Galsworthy passed, like Shaw, from the afternoon to the evening theatre. He attracted his public by his prestige as a novelist. He kept them there by giving them an entirely new experience.

Galsworthy was the first dramatist to achieve the complete realism which playwrights had been fumbling after ever since Robertson. He called it 'naturalism.' He explained his position in *Some Platitudes concerning the Drama*:

> The aim of the dramatist employing a naturalistic technique is to create such an illusion of actual life passing on the stage as to compel the spectator for the moment to lose all sense of

artifice, to think and talk and move with the people he sees thinking, talking, and moving in front of him. A false phrase, a single word out of tune or time, will destroy that illusion and spoil the surface as surely as a stone heaved into a still pool shatters the image seen there.

To do this the dramatist must eschew all artifice, discard the old dramatic trickery. William Archer amusingly described Galsworthy's attitude:

> Even the most innocent tricks of emphasis are to him as snares of the Evil One. He would sooner die than drop his curtain on a particularly effective line. It is his chief ambition that you should never discern any arrangement, any intention, in his work. As a rule, the only reason you can see for his doing thus and thus is his desire that you should see no reason for it.

Note that in this conception the creation of an illusion of actuality must be the work of the dramatist alone. He must not ask the audience to play the game of Let's Pretend, to collaborate by a "willing suspension of disbelief." He must achieve complete verisimilitude and thereby draw the spectator into the action of the play. His object, in scientific language, was to evoke a "participative empathy" and to shorten, if not abolish, the "æsthetic distance" between the audience and the stage. As this was a violation of æsthetic principles which had long been a basic convention of the theatre, it is worth a moment's examination.

'Empathy' is the psychologist's term for the body's instinctive imitative response to the contemplation of any object of interest. It is exactly what is implied by Galsworthy's phrase "to compel the spectator to think and talk and *move* with the people he sees thinking and talking and moving in front of him." The best illustration of this physical imitative reaction is to be seen at a boxing match, where the spectator is apt to be so far carried away by his excitement that he actually swings his fists, delivering imaginary punches. This may of course be only an uncon- scious impulse and if the restraints are greater than the stimuli he does not show it. "Æsthetic distance" is the attitude of detachment on the part of the spectator by which he reminds himself that he is contemplating a work of art and not a replica of nature. It is ensured by the unnatural material, the bronze or marble, of the statue; it is absent from the contemplation of a wax figure, which consequently disturbs by its reality. It is preserved by the frame around the picture; and in the theatre by the footlights and the proscenium arch, also by verse or by heightened speech. For an actor to step out of the picture in any way is to break the fundamental convention of modern acting. (This holds good of any form of theatrical entertainment, and its violation, for instance, by half-clad chorus-girls coming down into the auditorium and perching on the knees of elderly gentlemen in the stalls, however much it may please the "sat-upon," destroys true æsthetic enjoyment which demands a sense of unreality.)

There is a certain pleasure in empathic participation; it partly explains the fascination of watching games. But, according to the object of contemplation, it may become uncomfortable, as in the case of the empathic dizziness caused by the sight of a person perilously balancing on the window ledge of a skyscraper in the films, or even painful, as in the solitary confinement scene in Galsworthy's *Justice*, where it is intensified by silence so as to become almost unbearable. Both Grand Guignol and the thriller play have capitalized the mixed pleasure-pain effect of over-stimulated empathy, but this is a peculiar kind of enjoyment which is not æsthetic. In drama it should not be too much intensified or prolonged. Painful empathy can only be rendered æsthetically pleasurable in the theatre if the audience is lulled or hypnotized by some expedient such as verse or a repetition of words or phrases (a device much used by Maeterlinck). In this way the most revolting of all reactions, the response of the normal person to the emotion of horror, may even be made to assume a vaguely tragic beauty, a task attempted in *Salome* by that conscientious theorist and experimenter in æsthetics, Oscar Wilde. The point is that naturalism has no means of transforming or sublimating the painful, the ugly, the horrible.

At first Galsworthy's naturalism had the excitement of novelty. Describing the audience's reactions in his notice of *Justice*, Max Beerbohm wrote:

> The first-night curtain rises on the second act, and presently we have forgotten the footlights and are *in* a court of law. At a crucial moment in the cross-examination of a witness, somebody at the reporters' table drops a heavy book on the floor. An angry murmur of "Sh!" runs round the court, and we ourselves have joined in it. The jury retires to consider its verdict, and instantly throughout the court there is a buzz of conversation—aye, and throughout the auditorium too; we are all of us, as it were, honorary 'supers.'

In the same way, in the auction scene in *The Skin Game* the audience was made to feel itself *in* an auction room. In Basil Dean's production it was played with the auctioneer facing the audience and, as it were, eliciting bids from them so that they could hardly resist the temptation to join in the bidding on the stage. This, according to W.L. Courtney, was the supreme virtue of the naturalized drama: that "now and again it has the strange power to transport us out of ourselves. The audience becomes part of the play."

Now this meant a complete change in the attitude of the spectator to the play—the destruction of æsthetic distance made the spectator cease to judge it as a work of art or even as an entertainment. Once he was, so to speak, involved in it, he ceased to regard it as a play, but rather as an exhibition of reality. As P. P. Howe put it, "Galsworthy enters a theatre which for generations no man had thought he might enter without a clever plot invented or adopted, and proceeds to show us the peculiar interest of things which exist outside." At first it was a novel and amusing experience to pay half a guinea to be empanelled on a jury or to drop in at Christie's. The verisimilitude achieved had the novelty of the new Kodak snapshot camera. It showed up the falsifications of the conventional drama just as the snapshot's undeniable truthfulness made ridiculous the stiff and artificial poses of the professional photographer's "artistic" time exposures. But instantaneous photography was also instructive. It saw what the eye could not. For centuries painters had been painting running horses without discovering how the animal moved its legs. Replacing the imagination of the black-and-white artist in the newspapers, instantaneous photography gave startlingly revealing glimpses of behaviour in moments of crisis as it began to record pictorially the happenings of "human interest," the new shibboleth of popular journalism, which being interpreted meant other people's misfortunes (train smashes, fires, murder, and sudden death), fostering and catering for that ghoulish gluttony for disaster that has made the present-day news summary a chaplet of catastrophe. Its service was similar to that of naturalism on the stage which Galsworthy defined as "the swaying and focusing of men's feelings and thoughts into the various departments of national life," for the dramatic pivot of the naturalistic play was also human interest as distinct from heroic interest. It dealt not with man's noble failures and overweening aspirations, but with his ineffectual struggles, for it had now been generally ccepted that Man's tragedy was no fault of his own but the irect consequence of the thwarting of his instincts by the

stupidity and tyranny of society. The limelight was turned
from the hero on to the victim. This was not art for art's
sake, but art for humanity's sake. As nearly as possible it
ceased to be art at all.

And so the dramatic hero, who had started off as a rival
to the gods, after a continuous *dégringolade* down the stairs
of time, now reached the ground. Under the influence of
modern pessimism, admiration of man's potential divinity
had given place to pity resulting from the consciousness of
the essential identity of human beings. The dramatist,
following the novelist, began to study human nature from
the common specimens around him, much as a schoolboy
learns natural history by collecting caterpillars. In the hope
of discovering some basic truth he tried to paint an accurate,
realistic picture of the commonplace, for the modern method
of arriving at conclusions, of which the philosophical name
was Pragmatism, attached more importance to the banal
than to the exceptional, the unique. And so a record of
experience in a Bloomsbury lodging-house seemed to him
more valuable than an unauthenticated tale of Avalon.
H. G. Wells, writing of the modern novel in 1909, said:
"The essential characteristic of the intellectual revolution
consists in the reassertion of the importance of the individual
instance as against the generalization." In this way the
playgoer, like the novel-reader, was invited to find an
interest in any accurate, realistic picture of ordinary existence. He was like the holiday-maker at the seaside coming
out of the sunshine into the Camera Obscura and paying
his penny to see reflected on a white circular table the passing
crowd, which he could watch outside for nothing.

There is a certain fascination in any glimpse of life, as it
were, caught unawares. After a surfeit of stage 'high life'
the public found a novel enjoyment in convincing peeps
at ordinary existences, especially if the milieu was unfamiliar.

Diana of Dobson's in 1909 owed its success to a 'snapshot' scene of the dormitory shared by the saleswomen of a large drapery store. It made an impression because it struck true, although audiences were entirely ignorant of the conditions in such establishments, rather than because it drew attention to the restricted lives of underpaid shopgirls—which was the purpose of the authoress in writing the play. The drawback of naturalism was that it could never be an end in itself, but only a means to stir the social conscience, for almost inevitably the naturalistic play became a propaganda play, and equally inevitably it ended in an *impasse* or on a note of interrogation, dramatically both very unsatisfactory handicaps. And as the only emotion it provoked was pity, it was all very depressing. And the last thing a West End audience went to the theatre for was to be depressed. The quicker facilities of travel, the Twopenny Tube and the motor-car, had made it more than ever upper-middle class. The restriction of the size of the pit and the greater comfort and attractions of the new palatial theatres of variety had lowered its popular percentage. When the well-to-do residents of the spreading outskirts of the town came in to 'do a show' they were dressed for the occasion, even if they came by tube or bus. The rule of evening dress, now virtually obligatory in the dress circle as well as in the stalls, had begun to be respected even in the upper circle. The visit to the theatre was followed by supper at a restaurant with, almost invariably, champagne. It was, in short, a festive incursion. No wonder that half the London theatres were given up to musical comedy. The choice of a straight play was a matter of anxious thought. It depended on the Press notices of the play, and perhaps even more on the recommendation of some friend who had already seen it. In those days of active social life the power of this whispering propaganda was very strong. There was a fair-sized, scattered reservoir of keen playgoers, as distinct from theatre-goers, who were sorry to miss a good play. And among this clique, which favoured the intellectual drama, naturalism was in fashion from 1906 until about 1911. By that time this form of theatrical slumming has fallen out of favour.

Galsworthy gave the drama a sharp jolt along the road of representational illusion. Shaw proved that a static play composed almost entirely of argument might have quite unsuspected dramatic power. (The American actor, Richard Mansfield, rejected *Candida* when it was offered to him with the remark: "A play without any action except moving from a chair to a sofa and vice versa. Ye Gods and little fishes!") Harley Granville Barker combined Galsworthy's naturalism with Shaw's argumentativeness, following the latter into the thicket of the discussion play though with by no means the same arrogant insouciance as his master when he plunged into the jungle of incoherent talk in *Getting Married* and *Misalliance*; yet Barker did not share Shaw's deliberate object of converting the nation to his opinions. His was a smaller public because he made too great a demand on an audience's powers of concentration. He had not Shaw's trick of making argument palatable by first knocking them slap-happy.

The success of the Vedrenne-Barker seasons at the Court proved that there was a public for an intellectual theatre. But it was equally made clear that this was a limited public; that an intellectual play could not therefore count on a long run, and if it was to be a financially sound proposition it must be put on with actors who were content with a modest salary. The solution appeared to be a permanent theatre which would do what had been done at the Court and was in fact done at State-subsidized theatres on the Continent: in short, a repertory theatre. The cry for a National

Theatre was temporarily dropped in favour of this idea.
It was vaunted as a panacea for all the ills that beset the
English stage. A theatre with a stock company, presenting
for as long as they continued to attract a constant alternation
of intellectual plays would, it was thought, be self-support-
ing, and provide the two things the theatre chiefly lacked:
first, a practising school of acting for serious actors who
were being demoralized by the long-run system, and,
secondly, a springboard for the serious dramatist. In 1909
two managers decided to give the idea a trial. The experiments were instructive. Herbert Trench at the Haymarket
planned to alternate on these lines *King Lear* and Maeterlinck's *The Blue Bird*, but very soon reverted to the usual
'run' policy. The difficulties of a daily change from one
play to the other were too great in a theatre which had
neither the stage room nor the stage mechanism for repertory. His experiment proved only the impossibility of
running a repertory system without the facilities which no
existing London theatre could supply. The other adventurer
was the American impressario, Charles Frohman, known as
the Napoleon of the theatre. To him such practical difficulties were only made to be overcome. With the Napo-
leonic touch he opened a repertory season with the best that
money could buy, both in the matter of dramatists and of
cast. The four alternating bills were Galsworthy's *Justice*,
Shaw's *Misalliance*, Granville Barker's *The Madras House*,
and a triple bill by George Meredith and J. M. Barrie. The
result was a heavy financial loss. *Justice* alone was successful.
It is clear that Frohman's programme was much too highbrow. It was unfortunate that he should have chosen the
moment for his experiment when Shaw, his head turned
perhaps a little by his overwhelming and long-deferred
success, assumed that he could now afford to despise his
public, on the mistaken assumption that they would swallow

anything he put his name to; an impudence promptly
rebuked by the total failure of *Misalliance*. If anything was
proved it was the fallacy of the idea that the theatre public
will be beguiled by a playwright's reputation. It never
grants the dramatist an overdraft. Only the actor can draw
upon the credit of his past achievement. The failure of
Frohman's experiment also showed that there was only a
very restricted public for the discussion play and that it was
Galsworthy who had made the blue print for the modern
serious drama.

And so in London the idea of a repertory theatre died,
and the cry for a National Theatre was revived. In the provinces conditions were different. It was there, first in
Manchester, then in Liverpool, Birmingham, and Glasgow,
that the repertory theatre came into being. Provincial
audiences had no local pride and nothing on which to
expend it. They went to see the touring West End play
that had been hoisted into celebrity by the London Press,
but as these London 'successes' were often manufactured
and were generously interspersed with musical comedies
the keen playgoer was very irregularly provided for. It
was this minority that the provincial repertory theatres,
ignoring the support and the opinion of the romance-fed
general public, undertook to serve. With this restricted aim
they were careful to cut their coat according to their cloth;
cheaply priced seats and modest salaries were obligatory
for a commercially sound system. Upon this principal and
the hypothesis that there was an appreciable percentage of
people to whom art was meaningful and free thought welcome Miss Horniman, with the experience of the Abbey
Theatre in Dublin behind her, refitted a virtually derelict
theatre in Manchester in 1907 for the purpose of offering
them a vital and intellectual drama. A drink, it used to
be said, is the quickest way out of Manchester; a jocular

intimation of the necessity for some method of escape. The Mancunian intelligentsia, their eagerness for culture whetted by the drabness of their industrial habitat, had already found a more soul-satisfying vent than alcoholic oblivion in music. The excellence of the Hallé concerts had earned them a reputation second to none for musical taste. Now, given the opportunity of becoming the leaders of dramatic taste, they accepted Miss Horniman's offering in a spirit of almost Teuton earnestness. To them, as to the Germans—perhaps because there was a strong German element in Manchester —the theatre meant culture, not merely a eupeptic diversion for the tired business man.

One may reflect in passing on the influence of the feeding habits of a nation upon the nature of its drama. No German went to the theatre on a full stomach; he sustained himself in the intervals with sausages and beer. In Manchester high tea, which Pinero had suggested as a prerequisite to the elevation of the drama, was an established custom, and the patrons of Miss Horniman's misnamed Gaiety Theatre went with hungry stomachs as well as with hungry minds. This may account for St John Ervine's description of a typical repertory audience going to the theatre "as some Dissenters formerly went to chapel, woebegonely and as if they came to atone for lamentable sins."

Here at last was the opportunity for the dramatist with ideas.

Hitherto, the unknown playwright had been denied consideration unless he could persuade some manager that his work satisfied the supposed requirements of the London public. The best he could hope for was a single performance by the Stage Society. If, by virtue of his name and reputation, he succeeded in penetrating the defence line of the commercial managements, he either suffered, like Henry Arthur Jones, on more than one occasion, an instant and crushing defeat at the hands of a conservative public or, like Pinero, decided that discretion was the better part of valour and promptly executed a strategic withdrawal and rewrote his last act. The Vedrenne-Barker experiment was the first break through on a very narrow front. But though the intellectual theatre had been able to consolidate the position it had won, it had been unable to enlarge it for lack of a reserve. It was the mission of the provincial repertory theatres to build up this reserve. Leaving military metaphor, we may now consider their contribution to the advance of the intellectual drama.

In London the fashionable dinner-hour was now so late that the curtain-raiser had almost disappeared. In the provincial repertory theatre the would-be playwright had a chance to make a beginning with a one-act play and thus find out what he could do before attempting something bigger. The literary playwright groping his way to life was enabled to develop at leisure into the live dramatist expressing himself in literature. He accepted naturalism as his form, partly because the limited facilities of the repertory theatre denied him any extravagance in the matter of scenery or costume, and partly because he accepted Jones's dictum that the drama should be 'mainly and chiefly the art of representing English life,' and the tradition that the persons of the drama must have some genuine characterization, the plot some analogy to events of actual existence. For his subject matter he drew on the middle-class life around him. His function as a playwright, as he conceived it, was to say something, to attempt some criticism of life. And, having been brought up in an environment of Nonconformity which still cherished that Victorian attitude of mind, abominable to the new generation as embodying the twin vices of hypocrisy and philistinism, the local boys who wrote for the Northern repertories were doubly dyed with the rebelliousness that was infecting English youth. One might have guessed that they held it a sacred duty to pour ridicule on every form of middle-aged authority, particularly the parental; to satirize its pride in respectability, its greed of civic honours, its complacent money-worship; to pillory the paternal autocrat, the self-righteous "town scoundrel," and the smug employer of labour with his belief in the omnipotence of "brass." But they were not interested in social questions; neither was their public. It is noteworthy that Galsworthy's *Strife* was a complete failure in the industrial north. What stirred them was the repression of the individual by the conventions of a narrow-minded Puritanism. All the problems of morality which their fathers regarded as capable of only one solution they declared open questions. Was it wrong for a girl to run away from home? Not necessarily; it might show a fine independence, as in the case of Janet in *The Last of the de Mullinses*. Should the misfit in a money-grubbing world meekly accept the disgrace of his incompetence and the suppression of his individuality? St John Hankin impudently stated the case for the unchastened hero of *The Return of the Prodigal*. Must the girl who has taken a lover stand out for wedlock and the legitimacy of her child? Stanley Houghton daringly put the modern viewpoint in *Hindle Wakes*. The very titles of these plays were insurgent and provocative (*The New Sin*, *The Younger Generation*).

With what gusto and what skill these youngsters exploded the canons of their parents with adventurous thought! "Have these young playwrights all inadequate fathers?" some one asked. "Or can it be that the playwrights' fathers are unfortunate in their sons?" Here was vitality and humour and very effective satire. For the first time in ages the dramatic author had escaped from the dictatorship of the public's pleasure and could write to please himself.

A few London dramatists had given to the timorous problem play a documentary realism and a social significance.
The Lancashire School, to use an inexact but convenient
label, transformed it into a naturalistic comedy of manners.
Their impudent exuberance saved it from the pessimism
inherent in the Galsworthian drama. The two methods
were interestingly contrasted in *Hindle Wakes* and *The
Eldest Son*, produced in London in the same year (1912).
Both dealt with the same problem and found an identical
and unconventional solution. Their success was evidence
of the freedom the stage had gained in the matter of permissible material: of a new and important change in the
moral attitude of the public. For although to all appear-
ances it was the dramatist who, at long last, was shaping
the drama of the future, being bound as we are to recognize
that the public is always the fundamental condition of the
drama, we must necessarily conclude that the public attitude
had changed. By the early nineteen-tens it had accepted
and imperceptibly accustomed itself to naturalism. As the
creed of the naturalistic dramatist exacted a devotion to the
bare and explicit truth of human life and character, its new
criterion of a play was: does it ring true? The trend of
realism which had invaded the novel in the 'nineties and
given reading as well as writing an undertone of aggressive
earnestness that belied the prevailing trivial estimate of
fiction, had seeped prematurely into the theatre with *The
Profligate* (1889) and *Widowers' Houses* (1892); and ever
since, like the perpetually fluctuating, gentle current at the
bottom of the ocean, which those whose business is the
salvage of sunken vessels know as "scend," a relentless tide
that ceaselessly lifts and shifts the ponderous mass on the
ocean bed, crushing, crumpling, twisting, flaking steel plates
into rust and whittling timber into matchwood, the current
of naturalism had privily been breaking up the seasoned

hocus-pocus of the theatre; so that, all at once, as it seemed, though the process had been subtly going on for twenty years, romance and melodrama, and even tragedy, had become as outmoded as the frock-coat and the polka. One by one, playgoers became aware that they had made a sudden and irrevocable readjustment, like that of an Irish immigrant in New York or of a dowdy woman after a drastic change of fashion. Almost without being aware that they were doing it, the public had been throwing out the old conventions of the theatre just as they had got rid of the bric-a-brac, the heavy mahogany, the potted palms, and tasselled draperies in their homes.

It was a change of vital importance to the drama. The dramatist had helped to create it; he must now conform to it. Naturalism had come to stay. A while back it had been as generally objectionable as the smell of Virginian tobacco had been to nostrils accustomed to Turkish and Egyptian. But, once acquired, the habit proved very difficult to shake off. It has been an incubus to the modern dramatist who has vainly striven to escape it. For naturalism, as Chekhov said, "tends to destroy the inner profound emotions in its effort to mirror their outer manifestations."

VII

BEHIND THE CLOUDS

The Nineteen-tens

PROGRESS sometimes appears to operate with the ideal equalitarianism of the game of cricket. In the evolution of the theatre actor and manager, playwright and poet, scenic artist and stage mechanician, fashion houses and theatrical costumiers, had, each and all, their innings. Now, after a long wait in the pavilion, the intellectual dramatist was in and seemed set for a long stay. Alone the artistic theorist had been denied an opportunity. The term 'producer,' in the modern sense, was still unknown. What we call production the Victorians called stage-management. The triumph of the doctrine that art without thought is dead relegated the artist to a very subordinate position in the theatre, if he was not being altogether dispossessed by the second-hand furniture dealer; for the suburban interiors, solicitors' offices, etc. of the naturalistic intellectual drama would have put the scenic artist out of a job, if he had not had the perennial musical comedy as a stand-by.

The production theorist was, of course, the enemy of realism. William Poël had begun, as far back as 1880, to swim against the tide when he presented drawing-room comedies "without the vice of scenery" in Willis's Rooms n King Street. For twenty years, in his work for the Elizabethan Stage Society, he had identified his art with primitive resources. He had introduced the apron stage, and with a stage made as bare as possible had won the respect of the Shakespearian scholar by showing "how swift and passionate a thing, how beautiful in its variety, Elizabethan blank verse might be" if the imagination of the audience were freed from the distraction of realistic scenery. He had gained a small but ardent following.

Gordon Craig, on the other hand, the arch-enemy of the Realistic Theatre, had tried with small success to awaken interest in his ideas of suggestive, non-realistic decoration, interpretative lighting, and an *übermarionette* actor purged of egotism and subordinate to the producer. Only his mother, Ellen Terry, had given him the opportunity to put his ideas into practice. His *décor* for *The Vikings* and *Much Ado about Nothing* roused no enthusiasm. The theatre, Craig prophesied, with its realism, would "end in the music hall, for realism cannot go upwards, but always tends downwards. . . . Ariel is destroyed, and Caliban reigns." There was no man in the theatre, he complained in 1908, who was "a master in himself; no one capable of inventing and rehearsing a play; capable of designing and superintending the construction of both scenery and costume; of writing any necessary music, of inventing such machinery as is needed and the lighting that is to be used." And, finding himself without honour in his own country, the prophet of the absolutism of the producer who should co-ordinate all the contributory arts of the theatre went abroad to join the other prophets of a retheatralized theatre who, variously inebriated by Rheinhardtism, Moscow Art Theatre-ism and Russian Balletoxy, joyously hailed him as a leader and an inspiration. These all had one thing in common: they dreamed of a glorious blending in a fantastic non-realism of all the arts of the theatre. In England these separate arts still worked in watertight compartments. In the insular world of the London theatre the writings of Adolphe

Appia and Georg Fuchs which had started the Continental revolution were practically unknown. When Craig returned to England in 1911, the year of the publication of his book *On the Art of the Theatre*, the actor-knights were conspicuously absent from the banquet given in his honour although, in the words of Max Beerbohm's congratulatory message, "his influence is ubiquitous, festooned from point to point about Europe." By the actor-managers Craig was still regarded as a crank. When Tree, with some difficulty, was induced to invite his collaboration in a production of *Macbeth* his reluctance to efface himself entirely and meekly to deliver himself and his theatre into the hands of this uncompromising autocrat was made so obvious that Craig walked out in dudgeon.

It appeared that between them the thinkers and the actor-managers had driven Art into the wilderness. Almost alone of the practitioners of the London theatre, Harley Granville Barker had been absorbing the modern ideas which were electrifying the Continental theatre. Having been the foremost of the thinkers, he now allied himself with the artists. In 1912 he put on two almost futuristic productions of Shakespeare at the Savoy: the seldom-played *Winter's Tale* and the ever-popular *Twelfth Night*. London was startled in its insularity. His aim was to "subordinate details to a poetic whole." "I realize," he admitted, "that when there is perhaps no really right thing to do one is always tempted to do too much," adding the wish that people were not so easily startled. The 'decoration' of the plays was entrusted to Norman Wilkinson, to whom, quite unusually, large letter credit was given on the bills and programmes. Its "baroque eccentricity" lifted critical eyebrows and whipped the *Daily Mail* critic into a frenzy of derision. Barker swept all tradition overboard and gave imagination its head. The influence of William

Poël was evident in the use of a projecting apron stage covering the space customarily occupied by the orchestra; that of Craig in the uncompromisingly straight lines and hard rectangular contours of the stage architecture and in the abolition of the footlights. The stage was lit by lanterns projecting like guns all round the house, making the dress circle "look like a fortress." Even more revolutionary than the decoration in which a staring whiteness and sugar-icing pink were the dominant colours, set off by Noah's Ark trees of vivid green, were the costumes designed by Albert Rothenstein under the influence of Bakst. Shakespeare had always been dressed in some recognizable period, but Rothenstein's dresses were of no period at all. They were of *criard* colours, completed by strange plumed headgear, Christmas cracker crowns, and gold and silver boots. The whole production was a challenge to orthodoxy, an assertion of the claims of the producer, tired of being eternally twelfth man in the theatre-team and now determined to go in first. Barker ran the plays, like the Margate express, in two non-stop sections; with no cuts, except for the omission of four impossibly indecent lines from *The Winter's Tale*. The mesmerized audiences listened mouse-like during the performance and applauded generously at the end. The two plays were followed by a similar production of *A Midsummer Night's Dream*, with no Mendelssohn and instead of the traditional muslin-frocked juveniles, heroic gold-faced and gold-robed fairies that looked like Cambodian idols and postured like Nijinsky.

In this year Professor Gilbert Murray, obviously referring to Granville Barker, who had produced his translations of Euripides at the Court, declared in a Press interview: "The dramatic renascence inaugurated by Henry Arthur Jones and A. W. Pinero has spent its force, and bolder and more intellectual forces are giving rise to a new renascence." As a producer Barker was in the line of descent from Tom Robertson and W. S. Gilbert, with whom the play was the all-important thing. Their genius was in the executive ability by which they ensured their ideas being carried into action; ideas which were the product of a meticulous understanding of the result to be achieved. For this reason no actor ever failed in any of their productions. In his book *Early Stages* John Gielgud has given a graphic account of Barker arriving to rehearse a company after initial rehearsals conducted by a deputy.

> He rehearsed us for about two hours, changed nearly every move and arrangement of the stage, acted, criticized, advised, in an easy flow of practical efficiency, never stopping for a moment. We all sat spellbound, trying to drink in his words of wisdom and at the same time to remember all the hints he had given us, not one of which we had time to write down or memorize. Everything he said was obviously and irrefutably right.

This was in 1927, when the producer was the unchallenged cock of the walk and the actor reduced to as near the *Übermarionette* as he is ever likely to be; when Chekhov and the lesson of the Moscow Arts Theatre had reached the English theatre; when actors obediently followed chalk lines marked out on the stage and were content to be nagged or bullied into complete subordination to the idea of teamwork under the direction of the producer's master-mind. Thus the whirligig of time brings in his revenges. By that time the actor's wings had already been clipped by the author, whose copious explanatory directives kept him in tutelage. The characters of Shaw, Galsworthy, and Barrie are defined by their authors with such exactitude that they permit of only the smallest possible variety of interpretation.

In 1912, however, the actor-manager was in no hurry to surrender his sovereignty. It is doubtful if he even guessed that it was threatened. It was fortunate for the producers of the future that they had the provincial repertory theatres in which to learn their job and to experiment; in which they often had to do the work of designers, scene-painters, and electricians. The actor-managers basked in a prestige, an affection and esteem, which must not be thought of in terms of the hysteria that surrounds the modern film star. They were the heirs of Irving, the knights of an honoured profession. They had, in their way, the peculiar glamour which attaches to members of the Royal Family, a charm that owes as much to aloofness as to familiarity. As Desmond MacCarthy wrote of Tree, "Sometimes between the spectator and the actor there grows up a kind of one-sided personal relation, not merely an appreciation of the actor's art; it includes sympathy with the actor himself as he is conceived to be behind the parts he acts, and it may carry with it almost a delusion of intimacy." And at this time, with something of the same sense of obligation which makes royalty appear in the poorer districts of their cities and the remoter corners of their realm, the leaders of the London stage allowed themselves to be persuaded to appear in the provincial music-halls, thus giving a new life to the one-act play, which, being as it were the specimen vase chosen to exhibit a rare bloom, had to be a thing of exquisite workmanship. Linked with the names of playwrights of the calibre of J. M. Barrie, these quasi-regal tours brought the quintessence of the theatre to a new public and set the final seal of culture upon the aspiring theatres of variety.

As it happened, they were farewell bows to the great British public, for suddenly, in August 1914, came the *Gotterdämmerung*. Perhaps the war only hastened it, for the gods of the Edwardian theatre were old; they had reigned for a quarter of a century. Wyndham had been knighted in 1902, Hare in 1907, Tree in 1908, and Alexander in 1909.

Before the world had recovered from the war they were all dead. The war brought into the theatre a virtually new public: it "let loose," said Shaw, "an audience fifty years behind the times," a generalization neither truer nor fairer than his description of it as composed of "innocents (soldiers on leave) and squealing flappers." It is true that, compared with pre-war audiences, the masculine percentage was very much increased. The leaven of thoughtful femininity which had helped to put the Shavian theatre on the map was conspicuously absent. The serious-minded woman was far too busy with her increased domestic obligations, with Red Cross work, and the care of Belgian refugees, to have much time or inclination to take the theatre seriously. Already by 1912 she had lost her passionate interest in the theatre; she had absorbed from the intellectual drama all it had to give her. It had been inspirational to her intellectual emancipation. She was already studying a new thing called social science—it was said that 70 per cent. of the readers of Sidney and Beatrice Webb were women —and was eagerly investigating a new kind of semi-practical mysticism known as 'Higher Thought.' Already some years before the war, if we may believe a contemporary observer, Maeterlinck, Francis Stopford, Fielding Hall, and Father Benson were "somewhat by way of taking Bernard Shaw's place as the Society girl's priests and prophets." Shaw himself, in a contribution to *The Nation* in 1909, mentioned "a discussion in a club of very young ladies as to whether I could be more appropriately described as an old josser or an old geezer which ended in the carrying of an amendment in favour of an old bromide."

However the new audiences were composed, they had no trait uniting them except the common desire to find in the theatre a momentary refuge from the war. The war had so deeply stirred the nation's long-repressed emotions that the artificial emotional stimulus of the drama met with no response. The humour and humanity of *David Copperfield* fell as flat as the patriotic spectacle of *Drake*. Bewildered actor-managers tried everything in vain: plays with war in them: spy and Secret Service melodramas; plays with no war in them, sweet, idyllic romances. The return to the stage of the adored and adorable Lily Elsie, of *The Merry Widow* fame, in a 'legitimate' rôle as a runaway Irish colleen at the court of Charles II failed as dismally as the usually safe Pinero play at the St James's, even after it had been provided with an amended ending. The strain of the great European conflict soon made it evident how much the public were in need of light entertainment for solace and distraction. By the end of 1915 Tree and Alexander, tired of the unequal struggle, leased their theatres, and in August 1916 began at His Majesty's the five-year run of *Chu-Chin-Chow*, with its cunning mixture of music, stage realism, and art pantomime, its constantly refurbished, 'Folies-Bergèrian' mannequin parade in frocks remarkable for their bizarre and gorgeous colour schemes. It is easy to be 'superior' about *Chu-Chin-Chow*, but the audiences who attended its 2238 performances were not composed of morons. They did not go just to watch houris disporting themselves on the ruins of the British drama. It had charming light operatic music which has stood the test of time, in Courtice Pounds it had a singer who had not only a delightful, well-trained tenor voice but also a genuine comedic gift (a rare combination), and in Oscar Asche and Lily Brayton accomplished Shakespearian performers who by their presence and delivery could make tinsel seem like gold.

What the trench-weary soldiers wanted most was colour, an antidote to the deadening dreariness of mud and khaki, and new tunes which, played on the company portable gramophone in billets behind the line with an untiring repetition that would make the modern song-plugger green with envy, could by their sentimental associations conjure up the memory of those few, almost unbelievable, carefree nights in town. These were provided by the revues. Tree had instinctively seen the trend of the time when, early in 1915, he revived the glamorous Japanese melodrama, *The Darling of the Gods*, as "the nearest thing in my repertory to revue." There were the big spectacular revues at the Hippodrome and the Alhambra, and the little intimate revues at the Vaudeville. The little 'family party' revue which had its beginnings in *Potpourri* at the Avenue Theatre in 1899, "the kind of fun that is found at a fashionable supper-party," with its chaffing of eminent men and women of the stage, had been continued in a slightly different form by the Follies in 1907 in which the genius of H. G. Pelissier combined the family party frolic with a revival of burlesque in his famous Potted Plays. "Their fun," wrote Max Beerbohm, "has a savour of its own, a savour of high spirits running riot in sheer silliness of invention with yet an undercurrent of solid, sober satire"—which invites an *en passant* reflection that we have rather lost our native knack of high-spirited silliness, with a footnote on the original equivalence of the word silliness with happiness. It was C. B. Cochran and André Charlot, the latter long associated with the Alhambra in the conception of brilliant and artistic spectacle, who saw in 1916 that this recipé was peculiarly suited to the modern English taste. It had also the additional advantage, a very considerable one in wartime, of being able to dispense with expensive garniture of scenery and costume. The revues at the Ambassadors and at the Vaudeville became a standing dish till long after the armistice. They were irresponsible frivolities wedded to bright and catchy music. They gave the impression that the producer had collected a lot of clever people, given them an outline of scenes in which they could show their special talents, and pushed them on the stage with the injunction to do whatever they liked as long as they enjoyed themselves in doing it. Such witty and clever writers as Harry Grattan, J. Hastings Turner, Arthur Wimperis, Ronald Jeans, and Dion Titheradge provided thumb-nail satiric sketches taking off the foibles of the day. Besides discovering a wealth of artistic talent these Cochran and Charlot shows furnished the staple pattern for the intimate revue which has been followed ever since.

If *Chu-Chin-Chow*, revue, and farce—for example, the long-lived *A Little Bit of Fluff*, with its illusory suggestion of naughtiness and one solitary and by modern standards entirely decorous glimpse of a silk-clad, shapely leg—dominated the war-time theatre, it would be unfair to blame the innocents who enjoyed this light-hearted fare for a deterioration in public taste. What Shaw called "the starvation of the highbrows," attributing the setback to the lack of culture of the new audiences, was in fact the fault of the major dramatists, himself included, who, having in the decade preceding the war won supremacy in the theatre, when the war came, abdicated. Except for a one-act play from Galsworthy, they were silent. Barrie alone continued writing, and the public showed its taste by rejecting that popular author's strange aberration into revue and by flocking to his later play *Dear Brutus*. The reception of this and of Somerset Maugham's *Our Betters*—the only two plays of the war years with a touch of class—showed that the public could not be held wholly responsible for the eclipse of the drama.

Even more significant was the response to the valiant work at the Victoria Theatre, in the Waterloo Road, of Lilian Bayliss, who, against the advice of every manager in London, persisted in her policy of presenting Shakespeare at cheap prices. In due course she produced in succession all thirty-six first-folio plays and was rewarded by crowded houses. The army did more for the drama than the London managements. The first garrison theatre was opened at Oswestry by the G.O.C. Western Command in October 1916. It was built out of soldiers' funds. At the Armistice there were ten official companies performing plays to the troops. Whatever a later generation may choose to believe, the nation entered the war of 1914–18 in a very different spirit from that in which they found themselves involved in the war of 1939. It took up arms in both to honour its treaty obligations, but in the first the volunteer armies enlisted because they believed in the moral issues at stake. If a great dramatist had risen to the occasion, if the leaders of the theatre had aimed higher and not run away from life, the public would not have been found wanting.

The hard-won victory was welcomed by the nation in a solemnly idealistic and heroic mood, a fact obscured by the much-publicized Armistice-night demonstrations of hysteria in the West End of London. It believed in the slogans that crystallized its hopes of a better world and looked with confidence to the politicians who coined the slogans to carry out their promises. Even the Common Man 'thought big' under the ever-present reminder that the dead had given their lives for bigger things. In bigness was the League of Nations conceived. For the first time that now all too familiar and ironic cliché of the newspapers—the Big Three and the Big Four—burst into the headlines. And in the theatre, after a long absence, there was at last again a place for the hero on the stage. He made his appearance in 1919.

While the London theatre had been frolicking, the Birmingham Repertory Theatre under the guidance of its founder, Barry Jackson, had pursued its original policy of "serving an art instead of making that art serve a commercial purpose." With this object he put on plays of quality because he himself believed in them. This did not mean that Birmingham was especially artistic or enlightened. Except for the co-operation of a small number of well-wishers, Jackson himself declared the Repertory Theatre "was looked upon by the majority of the citizens, if they thought about it at all, as a freakish hobby with no purpose other than to find an outlet for superfluous time and money." It owed its ultimate success to the loyalty of its associates, its actors, and its dramatists, to their leader, and to the aim to do good things, labouring incessantly and striving constantly without thought of gain or exaggerated personal success. In 1902 Barry Jackson met John Drinkwater, then a clerk in the employ of the Birmingham branch of an insurance company, at some amateur theatricals, and Drinkwater became an actor, producer, and dramatist in the Birmingham Repertory Theatre. In 1918, at the psychological moment when the instinctive and abiding need for hero-worship had focused itself upon the leaders of the nations, Drinkwater, who had already achieved some reputation as a poet, gave Barry Jackson *Abraham Lincoln.* It came to London the following year and, after making a modest bow at the little Embassy Theatre, pursued a triumphant career from there to the Lyric, Hammersmith, and finally to the Lyceum, a most unsuitable theatre, for it was a new genre, a biographical play of quiet dignity and completely untheatrical, written for a little theatre. With a certain artlessness, which is perhaps the art which conceals art, Drinkwater showed his hero at six successive turning-points in his career—moments when it was necessary for him to make a vital decision, a decision affecting not only himself, but also the future of his nation. His portrait of Lincoln was faithful to the truth, if not entirely to the facts. Apart from the merits of the play its timeliness contributed to its success, for it was not surprising that the English, hypnotized by the *ex-cathedra* pronouncements of President Wilson into the belief that they had actually fought the war for the sake of democracy, a thing alien to both their traditions and rooted sentiment, should be attracted by this dramatic history of the great American democrat. It did, however, surprise the new London managements which after a brief emergence of the actress-manageress—there were no less than eight of them in 1918—were gradually coming under the control of the moguls of the big variety chains who imagined that they could grocerize the theatre. Startled by this symptom of intelligence in the public, they searched industriously for historic hero-dramas, and Lincoln was swiftly followed by Cyrano, Judith, Parnell, and Napoleon. But *Abraham Lincoln* was a swallow that did not make a summer. The decline in interest in leadership as a dramatic theme coincided with the perception that the stature of the builders of the future had been exaggerated.

The decade was not to close without a return of its leading dramatists to the theatre. Death had taken many of the most promising of the younger generation of playwrights; among them St John Hankin, Stanley Houghton, Harold Chapin, and the young poet, Elroy Flecker. Stephen Phillips too was dead. Shaw returned with *Heartbreak House*, which, though it contained perhaps more strictly original and penetrating thought than any of his plays, had a new underlying pessimism that ill accorded with the spirit prevailing at the time of its appearance. Moreover, Shaw, whose acceptance had never been truly national but only a class acceptance—and that the middle class—had dissipated much of its goodwill by talking a lot of what seemed to it mischievous nonsense about the war while it was still being fought. Galsworthy came back with *The Skin Game* in 1920, the usual scrupulously impartial study of a topical social phenomenon and a sermon on tolerance. It was Galsworthy *redivivus*, but Galsworthy unchanged. The theatre, a little bewildered by the arrival of the 'movies' which sealed the death warrant of melodrama and spectacle by doing them with an emotional and pecuniary recklessness the stage could not compete with, tried to pick up where it had left off. The survivors of the Old Guard on whom the mantle of leadership might have fallen, Fred Terry and Martin Harvey—two sleepy people, too much in love with the romantic to break away—set off once again for Wigan or Huddersfield with *The Scarlet Pimpernel* and *The Only Way*. The Benson and the Edward Compton companies resumed their plucky pegging away at educational Shakespeare. Granville Barker had retired to Gloucestershire. Gordon Craig has settled in Italy. The London theatre was left without a leader, without an inspiration. Where was the advance guard of the future?

VIII

FOG AND BRIGHT PERIODS

The Nineteen-twenties

IN the summer of 1919 the intelligentsia of the theatre held a meeting in Hampstead to discuss what Shaw called "the predicament of the theatre." Shaw himself was present. The old stormy petrel, Henry Arthur Jones, contributed his habitual flood of invective against "the speculative commercial manager now comfortably squatting with all the weight of his hoggish greed on the nearly lifeless English drama." As usual, somebody, this time Mr Robert Mac-Dermott, had a plan for an endowed theatre, which, if the requisite funds could be raised, he proposed to start building at Golder's Green Tube Station. The view taken of the theatre was, in the new parlance, a very 'highbrow' one, and it was unanimously decided that only a subsidizing of highbrowism could save the moribund drama from complete extinction by the commercialism of managers and the depravity of public taste. It was not suggested that either the dramatists or the acting profession were in any way to blame for its predicament.

As regards the depravity of public taste, despite the evidence that might have been adduced, the case was by no means proved. The defence might have quoted the reception of John Drinkwater's *Abraham Lincoln*, one of the few plays of high purpose written during the war, which aroused an immediate and unpredictable enthusiasm. Then,

again, there were the audiences at the Old Vic, "a crowd
of busy men and women determined to lay out leisure to
good purpose." They not only flocked to Shakespeare,
but when a series of afternoon performances of Professor
Gilbert Murray's translation of Euripides's *The Trojan
Women* was given there, "crowds gathered in the Waterloo
Road, trying to force their way into the overflowing
theatre and sat through the performance with patient
attention." The reception of the play encouraged Sybil
Thorndike to put on the *Medea* in the West End and
Euripides shared a triumph with a great tragedienne. The
Stage Society had had such success with the presentation of
Restoration comedy that a new society, the Phœnix, was
founded under its ægis for the production of Elizabethan
and Restoration drama. The Arts Theatre had discovered
Chekhov—if not yet the way he should be played. The
Curtain Group, the People's Theatre Society, and the
Independent Theatre were active and flourishing, the last-
named more so than it had ever been before. The Lyric,
Hammersmith, another playhouse off the map of Theatre-
land, was rapidly becoming a home for the intellectual.
The British Drama League held its inaugural meeting and
the first number of *Drama* appeared in August 1919. It is
clear that at the time of the Hampstead meeting the public
interest in the drama was far from moribund. Nor did it
lessen. In his survey of the theatre in 1923, the year he
became the dramatic critic of *The Sunday Times*, James
Agate wrote:

> Never, it must be said firmly, has the theatre loomed more
> largely in the public consciousness than during 1923. Reper-
> tory theatres have sprung up in two important centres, Oxford
> and Bristol; those at Birmingham and Liverpool have gone
> from strength to strength, while even defunct Manchester
> has been heard knocking on the coffin lid. Playgoers' clubs

and debating societies have had unparalleled attendances. At least one firm of publishers has devoted a large proportion of its output to works connected with the drama. The younger Sunday evening theatres—Repertory Players, Play Actors, Fellowship of Players—have shown astonishing enthusiasm; the Phœnix Society has done brilliantly, while the comparative inactivity of the Stage Society has been, I will presume, only a collecting of strength for the fine programme now promised us in the immediate future.

Nor could a wholesale condemnation of the commercial theatre be reasonably substantiated. The commercial manager of the early nineteen-twenties was no more an enemy of art, a strangler of infant drama, than at any other time. The theatre-manager is a business-man, but he may also be an artist. It was the commercial enterprise of Sir Oswald Stoll which brought the Diaghileff ballets to the Coliseum, where a seat in the gallery cost eightpence and where they had been playing to packed houses for eight months at the time of Hampstead meeting; a further vindication of public taste. In the early 'twenties, thanks to the artistic enterprise of C. B. Cochran, London had an opportunity to see the great Italian tragedienne, Eleanora Duse. He also gave it a Guitry season and brought over *Anna Christie* from America. Basil Dean, who came to London from the Liverpool Repertory Theatre, full of ideas of modern production methods, staged the late Elroy Flecker's poetic drama *Hassan* and Karel Capek's *R.U.R.*, and Nigel Playfair revived Gay's *Beggars' Opera* and put on Drinkwater's *Robert E. Lee* and the Capeks' *The Insect Play*.

On every side, both among the public and among those who provided for it, there was evidence of an eager curiosity about the drama, a desire to make the theatre more than a mere place of entertainment. The body of serious and intelligent playgoers was still of course, comparatively small and artistic idealism had not infected the bulk of theatre managements, but there were at least half a dozen groups of able men and women, somewhat disunited, it is true, with a notion of an ideal to be followed. The vestal flame nourished by the Stage Society for over a quarter of a century had not spread into a blaze, but it had kindled other fires. Its work had been achieved.

If there was a keen public for Shakespeare and Chekhov, for Greek and Elizabethan and Restoration drama, not by any means always ideally performed and without the added attraction of box-office names, and also a lively interest in the experimental work of Continental playwrights, how was it that there was not an efflorescence of native drama? It is a difficult question to answer satisfactorily. The reason seems partly to seek in the snobbism—or is it perhaps a national artistic inferiority complex?—of the highbrow intellectual. James Agate clearly made this charge:

> If I repeat the old commonplace that the way in which to get the best out of a West End piece is to leave your intelligence at home, it is because I want to fasten the blame on to the proper shoulders, those of the 'intellectuals' on both sides of the curtain, who, in this country, do the serious theatre much harm. Go to Hampstead and you will find a lot of moping owls complaining in whispers and horn-rimmed spectacles of the Decay of the Drama. It is for these sad followers that the Repertory playwright bedews his tearful manuscript, presenting life as though it were a passage from the womb to the grave, so short, as Stevenson says, as to be "hardly decent and with no time at all for joy."

On the one hand, there was the popular playwright who rushed to the opposite extreme, pretending that life was a continual *thé dansant* and who was "so contemptuous of his public that he deemed it incapable of being tickled or thrilled by any matter above the comprehension of a nursemaid": on the other, the 'intelligent' dramatist, "too arrogantly absorbed in his cerebrations to care what sort of entertainment he provided in the theatre." There were a few brilliant exceptions, playwrights who had something to express and had taken the trouble to master its expression, but somehow the interest in the drama of the intellectual public did not appear to embrace the living dramatist. They seemed to mistrust a playwright who was not either dead or foreign. If Allan Monkhouse, said Agate, had been a Russian and his name Monkoussikoff his work would create a furore. One unknown playwright actually succeeded in obtaining production and critical applause for an original play by the trick of pretending that it was in fact a translation from the German; a hoax which profited him nothing when the cat was let out of the bag.

The reluctance of the intellectual dramatist to acquire the technique of the theatre was largely the fault of Shaw's example. In *Getting Married*, and still worse in *Misalliance*, he had through laziness or indifference abused the licence generously vouchsafed to his garrulity on the condition that he amused. In these plays he had failed to keep his part of the tacit bargain. He had showed too clearly his contempt for the public that applauded him. He made no effort in either to shape their continuous and incoherent conversation into a play. Over-confident of his ability to talk the devil out of the liver wing of a turkey, as they say in County Cork, or too intent upon converting the nation to his opinions, he let his addiction to palaver run away with him. And the theatre public decided that all talk, even Shavian talk, and no play made George a dull boy. As a result, in spite of his European reputation, his almost legendary prestige, and his influence on the thought of the pre-war generation, the Sage of the Adelphi had to a great extent dissipated the goodwill of his English theatre-going public.

This was also part of a general tendency to regard all pre-war dramatists as back-numbers, or "Forerunners," as Ashley Dukes called them in his book *The Youngest Drama*.

When in 1919 Shaw published *Heartbreak House* without waiting for a production, he could afford to dispense with the theatre. He had first started writing for the stage because he needed it as a platform; it was the best available means of converting the nation to his opinions. ("I have no other object in writing plays," he told the Parliamentary Committee on the Censorship of Plays.) Now he could reach a world-wide audience through the medium of print. He could do without the theatre. All his post-war plays, with the exception of *St Joan*, belong to literature rather than to the drama. It seems more from force of habit than for any other reason that they took dramatic form. Shaw chose to remain a brilliant sun illuminating the theatre, but aloof. It cannot rightly be said that he inspired the post-war dramatist, but the modern playwright, bumping along the dusty, narrow lanes of Galsworthyshire, could not help being conscious of his Mephistophelian grin reflected in the driving mirror, daring him to open up the throttle. And very few besides Priestley and Bridie have been bold enough to accept the challenge.

The post-war serious playwright has never been able to find the exit from naturalism. His play pattern is still the Galsworthy-Stanley Houghton drama. The Youngest Drama has never quite succeeded in escaping from the influence of the Forerunners, which has rather weighed upon it. Shaw encouraged the playwrights who came after him in the belief that discussion could be a substitute for action. The Galsworthian example made him chary of whole-hearted emotion. Galsworthy's judicial restraint, his detachment, his exact balancing of more than a single emotional appeal—and this is true of plays made on his pattern, like Clemence Dane's *A Bill of Divorcement* as well as of his own *The Skin Game* and *Loyalties*—restrain, detach, and thereby exhaust an audience. There was a loss of emotional warmth in the post-war theatre. It was partly due to the dramatist, partly to the actor, and partly to the audience. The blight of naturalism had also settled on the actor. There were perfect actors in the 'twenties but no great ones. The perfection of Charles Hawtrey and Gerald du Maurier, who had set the fashion, was the faultlessness of the miniature method. The natural drawl, the very lack of exaggeration, and the suave power of suggestion by the mere lifting of an eyelid were exquisite but cramping. Their example led to a loss of breadth as well as depth in acting, and by reaction to a sudden admiration on the part of the public for the art of the clown, and to a vogue for farce. This natural style of acting also affected the playwright because these actors took no risks, asking nothing of a part except the question, "Does it suit me?"

The change in the constitution of audiences also had some share in this loss of warmth. St John Ervine attributed it to the contraction or abolition of the pit (which Agate called "the soul of the playhouse") and to the fact that the comparative discomfort and cost of the theatre had driven the young to the cinema. "Quick and responsive youth in the pit," he declared, "sent a feeling across the less ardent stalls to the stage which heartened and roused the players."

One way or another the theatre was being starved of its most needful food: emotion. The public still enjoyed the luxury where they could find it: in the frank sentimentalism of *Polyanna* and in the easy religious emotionalism of *The Wandering Jew*, a spectacular play which astutely combined its religious appeal with lurid and alluring pictures of unchristian depravity on the approved model of Wilson

Barrett's old money-spinner, *The Sign of the Cross*, and in which the author, like Mrs Siddons at the dinner-table, continually lapsed into unintentional blank verse. The plays of the 'twenties did not touch the deep emotions. George Santayana, who visited England at this time, found English plays too transparently moral, sentimental, or intellectual. The serious theatre was willy-nilly committed to intellectualism. The other two vices, however, inherited from the Victorian age and deep-ingrained in our national character, the post-war generation was strenuously determined to eradicate; particularly every sentimental weakness. Lytton Strachey set a fashion by 'debunking' the eminent Victorians. The 'bright young things' of society ran wild, like precocious, impudent children, parading the heartlessness of youth and betraying in their speech, behaviour, and relationships a distrust for sentimentality that amounted almost to hatred. Disrespect for age and moral authority found its immediate expression in a casually intolerant attitude towards parents, reflected in many plays. The mask of impassiveness they had encouraged their sons to wear was now adopted by their daughters. These young eggs took a special pride in appearing 'hard-boiled.' Even in the free and unchaperoned association of boys and girls which the war had made unexceptionable the worst of bad form was any tendency to 'sloppiness.'

This cultivated cynicism found its expression on the stage, exasperating the old, embarrassing the middle-aged, and delighting the young. It shocked the elder by its deliberate heartlessness. It can be found well represented in a sketch in the Charlot revue *London Calling* in 1923, a revue which drew attention to the multiple talents of its part-author who also sang, danced, and acted in it besides composing lyrics and music. The name of this versatile young actor was Noel Coward. In this sketch a Mrs Poppie Baker (played

by Gertrude Lawrence) is rung up in the early morning
while she is still in bed to be told that her husband has
jumped off Waterloo Bridge. Though secretly pleased at
the news she proceeds to ring up all her friends, and, acting
the state of devastation appropriate to a tragically widowed
wife, makes appointments with each at Ciro's. Then the
telephone rings again. The report of her husband's suicide
was a mistake. Her language is cut off by the fall of the
curtain. 'Bright Young Thingery' had made its irruption
into the theatre. This witty and cynical sketch was not only
an instance of the eternal purpose of the clever young man
to *épater le bourgeois*; it reflected the cynicism of the age.
In the same way Noel Coward's first full-length comedies
were more than just insolent toots on youth's reckless
motor-horn. They were a comedy of manners, if, as some
said, only of bad manners. And they brought back into the
theatre something it seemed in danger of losing in its inexpert intellectualism or its contemptuous triviality: speed,
wit, and technique. It was at once apparent that he knew
his business as a dramatist, and that even if he was intent
on being amusing he was also trying to draw real people.
If his characters were second-rate people, it was because he
saw people as second-rate; in the same way as his snappy,
colloquial dialogue was the common speech of his contemporaries. His plays, it is true, were only a picture of a
limited section of society; they presented only one facet
of the truth of changing life. But truth is like the sun.
Sunshine is very pleasant with the sun ninety million miles
away. When Coward or any of the younger dramatists
tried to stir the deeper emotions or probe the malady of the
age—as he did in *The Vortex*, and as did Van Druten in
After All, Miles Malleson in *The Fanatics*, and, most relent-
lessly of all, Somerset Maugham in *For Services Rendered*—
the public could not take it. They winced under the

burning glare of truth, thereby showing that there was some justification for Noel Coward's petulant complaint that "the middle class are incapable of *really* enjoying anything but the blatantly obvious, and the farther it is removed from truth, the better they like it." This is the reason why Maugham gave up writing for the stage. In England even the most accomplished playwright has failed when he spoke the truth too brutally—though for some extraordinary reason foreign authors, from Strindberg to Tennessee Williams, have been able to do this with success. If high jinks and trite sentimentality have been the staple of Coward's later work it was because he knew only too well which side his bread was buttered.

The middle 'twenties were boom years. Money was plentiful and there was a spirit abroad of "let us eat, drink, and be merry." If it was vaguely guessed, even then, that the world was heading for the rocks, the prevailing reaction was: What the heck? The playgoing public, at any rate, spending its easy money on farce, the lightest of comedy, revue, and American musicals, wanted less than ever to think or to be preached at. Nor did it want to be deeply moved. The brief interest in the classics swiftly waned. The sudden enthusiasm for Elizabethan and Restoration drama soon petered out. Shakespeare entered upon a period of almost unparalleled neglect, and, partly, no doubt, as a result of the recognition that he once again spelt ruin, he was never more inadequately staged or performed. It seems as if the springs of deep emotion had been atrophied; the young playwright, if he felt it, strangled it at birth. A young emotional actress was such a rarity that Meggie Albanesi, whose Sidney Fairfield in Clemence Dane's *A Bill of Divorcement* was perhaps the only great emotional performance of the 'twenties, left behind a memory unique in the history of the theatre; for she died at the age of twenty-four, her physical powers exhausted by the intensity of her emotions.

Even musical comedy, that hitherto reliable medium for nostalgic and sentimental indulgence, was in process of changing its character entirely. The dynasty which began with *The Geisha*, with its strange idealism of miscegenation and its Cook's tours of the glamorous Orient, and the succeeding Viennese operetta, in which true hearts were more than crowns and true love thwarted the marriages of convenience arranged by Ruritanian royalties, gave place to transatlantic importations in which sentiment only obtruded apologetically into farce and romance was treated with a 'cissy derision.' This phrase is that of the American critic, George Jean Nathan. The soubrette and the comedian dispossessed the prima donna and the matinée-idol tenor, for dancing had taken precedence over singing. Slickness, speed, rhythm, and syncopation concealed their emotional deficiency. In the attempt to emulate *No, No, Nanette* the English musical romantic play disappeared. Our musical comedy purveyors rushed into furious imitations of American successes and in them the fount of native wit and melody ran dry. The tide of vacuity swamped A. P. Herbert's brave attempt to re-create an English comic opera. Here was a Gilbert; but alas! there was no Sullivan.

Another normal, perennial playgoing appetite refused to be denied: the appetite for sensation. More people go to the theatre for some kind of thrill than the many who go merely for amusement and the few who go to think. But people's sensations like their emotions had become blunted. In a world that had lived through the war of 1914–18 sensationalism in the theatre had grown immensely more difficult. Moreover, the cinema, in process of killing emotion by its treacly overstressing of pathos, indulged in the wildest sensationalism. In this it could clearly outdo the theatre.

There was, however, one form of sensationalism in which the theatre had, and still has, the advantage. Literature can do it still better; for to achieve its full effect it must play on the imagination. The Victorians knew it as the "shilling shocker," their errand boys as the "penny dreadful." Modern playgoers know it as the "thriller play." Our addiction to it can only be explained by our inability to be thrilled by anything but violence. Or must we seek the explanation in some sadistic human instinct which must needs find relief in one way or another, for we, the least violent of European nations, are alone in our delight in the thriller play. The Continental theatre rejects it unequivocally. When the dramatic version of Bram Stoker's vampire horror-story *Dracula* first toured the provinces in the nineteen-eighties a trained nurse went with the company to administer restoratives to members of the audience whose nerves were insufficiently robust to stand the suggestion of terror. When R. L. Stevenson collaborated with W. E. Henley in *Deacon Brodie, or The Double Life*, in 1884, the *Saturday Review* attributed its failure to "an overstrained prolongation of febrile stimulus." In forty years British nerves had been toughened. It was precisely on this that the thriller play relied. It is psychologically true that terror— or, indeed, any form of pain—may be intensified to a point at which it becomes pleasurable. Psychologists tell us that in extreme cases of fascination, as when a man is attacked by a tiger, this factor in terror, by being the predominant one, even lends it something of the complexion of pleasurable excitement. According to Aristotle, fear is an essential ingredient of tragic spectacle. It is, however, otiose to embark on any æsthetic or psychological examination of the thriller; for although the primary object of this kind of play is to evoke this sole emotion of terror it is not to be supposed that any spectator really feels it. On the contrary, he will call a good thriller great fun; so oddly do we misuse our words denoting mirth. It is, in fact, a game, as watching a thunderstorm was to the child, Walter Scott, who was found lying on his back on a hill-top clapping his hands and crying "Bonny, bonny!" at every flash of lightning. The author's part in the game is to observe all the improbabilities and to excite at unexpected moments the somatic responses of terror, to make the spectator jump by sudden blood-curdling shrieks or the headlong fall of rigid corpses out of suddenly opened cupboards.

This flirting with make-believe terror as an unadulterated form of theatrical entertainment was first introduced in the 'twenties when the Thorndikes tried to establish an English Grand Guignol at the Little Theatre. But Grand Guignol with its insistence on the horrific and the macabre has never become acclimatized in England. The horrible on the stage is necessarily visual, and if it does not horrify it is ridiculous by its excess of extravagance; or, if it does, it grazes too nearly the brink of horror and of all that would in actual realization be most repulsive. The thrillers of Edgar Wallace only played the terror game, which is not the same thing. As it became increasingly popular it began to be varied with the mystification game, the game of "spot the criminal." The mystery play—in a sense very different from the original meaning of the term—reappeared as a distinct dramatic species. The only curious thing about it was that it deliberately broke what had always been considered one of the first rules of drama: that the playwright must keep no secrets from the audience. Even William Archer succumbed to the lure of this new game. Rather surprisingly, the veteran critic and Ibsenite brilliantly concocted out of the rag-bag of old Victorian melodrama the taut and gripping thriller *The Green Goddess*, which ran for 416 performances and showed that in skilful hands the thriller could be made plausible, that the game could be played by academic rules. Then suddenly life caught up with fiction; the most lurid imagination of the thriller writer was outdone by fact. The emergence of gangsterism in Chicago and the fame of Al Capone gave *On the Spot* almost the realism of a Freudian character study.

It was not in the thriller nor in the comedy of the Noel Coward school that the aspiring actor could learn the higher proficiency of his art. Fortunately for the stage of to-day there were the repertory theatres. Most of the present generation of actors served their apprenticeship in them or else were actively connected with the young play-producing societies. The repertory theatres had not yet been forced by economic pressure to depend for support on the latest London successes, as they did when they multiplied and the arrival of the talking picture offered a formidable competition. They were still able to follow artistic ideals, and their young actors were infected by them. The young actor was a much humbler person than he had yet been in the history of the theatre. He had a less egotistic notion of his art. He was more amenable to 'production,' more ready and willing to subject himself to a thought-out conception of the play's proper total effect. The repertory theatres had in fact become, or were becoming, what the Continent called Art Theatres, of which the most widely known examples were the Theatre du Vieux Colombier in Paris, and the Moscow Art Theatre. In these the autocracy of the producer demanded implicit obedience. It was its aim to interpret—with, in Jean Cocteau's phrase, an "incredible disinterestedness"—the author's purpose and the pattern of the play. The greater individualization of the minor characters in the modern play made small parts more grateful to the actor. At the same time it was more important that their interpretation should be rightly subordinated to the whole.

Production was no longer merely a matter of seeing that the lesser fry were never more prominent than the leading man or lady. Indeed, in the new drama it was often difficult to assess the lead. This was particularly true of Chekhov, whose belatedly discovered plays now began to figure largely in almost every repertory, and highly tested the producer. Though production in England had been advancing rapidly since the beginning of the century, it was still, more or less, an infant art. As the producer learnt his business of coping with the 'atmospheric' play he rose in dignity in the hierarchy of the theatre. Under his baton the actors became the members of an orchestra and himself alone the exponent of the creative mind. In many ways this was an immense improvement. Among other things it gave the scenic artist a new conception of his work, and he, too, rose correspondingly in dignity. He was no longer called upon simply to furnish a striking and effective background for the play—'furnish' is the apt word, for stage sets had grown more and more to resemble the show windows of the Tottenham Court Road. It was now his task to provide an imaginative setting which should serve to support the text and create a congruous atmosphere. 'Atmosphere,' like 'orchestration,' was almost the be-all of production. Not unnaturally at first both the scenic designer and the producer, whose intentions he carried out, were tempted into an over-use of atmospheric devices to the distraction of attention and the destruction of dialogue—a temptation made easier by the introduction of a new producer's toy, the Schwabe-Hasait lighting. But this was only the pardonable extravagance of the beginner. The young English producers, like the young English actors, were very eager to learn. Such distinguished foreigners as Komisarjevsky and Michel Saint-Denis taught them much. They soon ruled in their own right. Their expertness was a great encouragement to the dramatist, for with provincial, Continental, American, radio, and motion-picture rights a play was potentially a very valuable property and a great deal depended on the excellence of its original production.

IX

THE CLIMATE CHANGES

The Nineteen-thirties

THE world economic collapse of 1929 brought the jazz age abruptly to a close; the age of which Noel Coward had been at once the spokesman and the satirist was at an end. He, like his generation, had been at one moment dazzled by the smarter aspects of its 'sophistication,' at others nauseated by its emotional and spiritual nihilism. Let him analyse the attitude of those lost children of the war, for who could do it better? In his most serious play, *Post Mortem*, one of the characters, driven by it to the contemplation of suicide, explains it thus: "a sort of hopelessness which isn't quite despair, not localized enough for that. A formless, devastated boredom, everything eliminated, whittled right down to essentials which aren't there." Or shall we quote from fiction? Soames Forsyte's daughter, Fleur, typical of her generation, exclaims: "Life! Oh! Well, we know it's supposed to be a riddle, but we've given it up. We just want to have a good time because we don't believe anything can last. But I don't think we know how to have it." The grim nineteen-thirties crashed into this epoch of sterility like an iceberg into a liner on a luxury cruise. Boredom gave place to apprehension. Stark and disintegrating facts loomed suddenly out of the cold fog of vague disquietude. At home unemployment had risen to the two million mark, the churches were losing influence and politicians had forfeited confidence, the marriage code was largely in process of breaking down, and economic insecurity made marriage more and more impossible for those with uncertain incomes. Abroad, another European war was just around the corner which might or might not be averted and in which we might or might not be involved. France had shown her faith in the prospect of peace by beginning to construct the Maginot Line. England tried to isolate herself by buying British, by the conversion of the domestic debt, and by erecting a tariff wall around the empire. The epidemic of nationalism, poisoning the European atmosphere, infected England with a mild attack of Kiplingism.

It was at this juncture that Coward produced *Cavalcade* at Drury Lane in 1932. In this sentimental scrap-book of thirty years the professed arch-antisentimentalist, having prepared the ground for his apostasy by the prettiness of *This Year of Grace* and the romanticism of *Bitter Sweet*, indulged in an unashamed nostalgia for the once derided values of the bourgeois Edwardians. The public went for it like hungry urchins let loose in a confectioner's shop. Our congenital sentimentalism, suppressed by the sophistication of the 'twenties, burst out into a rash. But it was a sentimentalism mixed with national pride, a kind of penitence for having lost faith in ourselves, of having been disloyal to our heritage. With masterly showmanship Coward utilized the vast stage of the Lane as it had been used in the old days of Drury Lane melodrama, which had achieved success largely by the intuitive skill with which its compilers fulfilled the fantastic wishes of its audience. In those happy days the spectator had vicariously hunted with the Quorn, played polo at Hurlingham, gambled at Monte Carlo, won the Derby, driven the first motor-car, and flown the first aeroplane. Now, reliving the past, embarking for South Africa, toasting the birth of the new century, mourning the passing of the Queen, and marching once again through Flanders mud, he left the theatre in a state of grace, with a sense of dignity retrieved.

Such is the power of 'good theatre.' No one pretended that *Cavalcade* was more than this. No one claimed that it was great drama. It was aimed at and was acclaimed by the most conventional of publics. This relapse into the darling vice of sentimentalism soon set the highbrows buzzing. For a while a minor battle raged. Agate attacked them in an article entitled *Swat that Wasp*, and Sean O'Casey characteristically poured his scorn on the Pontiffs of the Theatre who "dislike drama which has the heart-beat of life in it, and treat a play which has the sound of flutes as if it were a mendicant at a street corner begging a coin from cold pockets."

Not that the sound of flutes was anywhere evident in the plays of the early 'thirties. There were no flautists—if we except O'Casey himself—among the rising dramatists. Rodney Ackland in *Strange Orchestra* and Ronald Mackenzie in *Musical Chairs* had attempted a little Chekhovian chamber music, but for the most part the wood-wind was drowned by the "subhumanities of Mayfair backchat, or the domestic parrotings of suburbia." Was the heart of life still beating in the theatre? If by that is meant, as the highbrows understood it, was the dramatist seriously trying to bring his audiences face to face with some side or other of an urgent contemporary problem, the answer is no. Playwrights showed little sign of being affected by the new gravity and sense of responsibility which was remarkable in the young poets of the time. They had, it is obvious, to attract a different public, a public "fed for so long on the pap-diet of light comedies and crook plays that it was doubtful if its stomach could stand anything stronger." But there was a more cogent reason for their timidity in handling themes that mattered. Although there was an audible demand for plays of 'social significance' there was a prevalent idea that such themes were propaganda. And, as the critics were always insisting, propaganda was not art. A test case was *Love on the Dole*, a piece of conventional naturalism showing the miseries of economic insecurity. When it was produced in 1934 the public stayed away; not because the play was painful, but because the immediate reaction was that unemployment was not a subject for the theatre. It was nursed into a success only because it had strong financial backing. At about the same time a play, *Sunshine House*, which dealt movingly and excitingly, as well as with an astonishing amount of humour, with the conditions of privately run mental-homes and the law on the certification of the insane, despite high critical praise both for the play and for the acting, had to be withdrawn because the backing was insufficient.

There was also another deterrent to the playwright: the censorship; not so much its activity as its mere existence. It had recently banned *Young Woodley*, a sincerely written play about a schoolboy's adolescent infatuation for his housemaster's wife, and then removed the ban after the play had run for twelve months in New York. *Victoria Regina* was played for two years in America before it was licensed for the English stage. Plays about Parnell, Gladstone, and Oscar Wilde had been forbidden. The capriciousness of the censorship was a boon to the little club-theatres now springing up. They were outside its jurisdiction. By the performance of forbidden plays they gained a welcome prestige in addition to the free publicity which is always the perquisite of the prohibited, and thus they created, perhaps beneficially for the future of the drama, a kind of adult playgoing aristocracy in their membership. But a club theatre with a seating capacity of two hundred or thereabouts was not much use to the professional playwright, who could ill afford the risk of having his work nullified by the veto of an official whom he could neither question nor oppose.

Among the plays banned about this time was one, *Red Sunday*, dealing with the Russian revolutions of 1905 and 1917. The censorship had always been a little touchy in the matter of plays with political ideas. In 1912 it had actually banned a play indirectly advocating socialism. It may perhaps be difficult to realize how acute was the conflict of political ideas in the 'pink decade' of the 'thirties. It was even suggested by some that *Cavalcade* revealed a Fascist mentality; but whatever slight resemblance there may have been between the mild access of patriotism with which Noel Coward's play so happily coincided and the jingoism of the Kipling furore of the eighteen-nineties, *Cavalcade* was in no way provocative. The success of the play and that of Kipling's writing uncovered the same modern tendency: the desire of people to escape from themselves in collective action, their prostration before the idea of the community, what Kipling called "the law of the pack." Hilaire Belloc, lamenting the loss of religion in an article on *The Modern Man* in 1936, wrote:

> Since a man must worship something there has been sub-
> stituted for his ancient worship the worship of the community
> of which he is a member. There has arisen a new religion
> which is not exactly the worship of the State but the worship
> of the collective body (formerly called England, now quite
> commonly called 'the Empire') of which the individual is a
> member.

Whether the collective body should take a Fascist (in the sense that Fascism was an order and a restoration) or a socialist form was a question of very vexed opinion. The stage was not the place to argue it. Shaw had the greatest difficulty in finding a theatre for his 'political fable,' *On the Rocks*. But it did find expression, on the one hand, in a resurrection of the past, a wistfulness about the good old pre-war days (as in *Cavalcade*); on the other hand, in an aggressive 'agitational theatre.' The latter began with a group of politically minded amateurs who called themselves "The Rebel Players" but who, in 1936, took a church hall in King's Cross which they renamed the Unity Theatre. The success of a political pantomime, *Babes in the Wood*, presented at Christmas 1938, sent its membership up to 7000. The Unity Theatre Society, Ltd, registered as a properly constituted Co-operative Society, was to be a "People's Theatre," taking its place "in the people's struggle against Fascism." It was imbued with "social purpose," and its plays all had "a message," usually expressed with the *naïveté* inseparable from the propaganda play. The Right had no theatre of its own, but in 1934 Colonel Blimp appeared as a dramatist. The success-story of Walter Reynold's melodrama, *Young England*, is surely unique in the annals of the theatre. Possibly encouraged by the reception of *Cavalcade* in the belief that the way of salvation both for the stage and for the country lay in the recovery of the lost downright emotions of his own youth, the aged author—he was eighty-three—concocted for the edification of young England a "real palpitating human drama, full of tears, love, laughter, and adventure," and, incidentally, permeated with the most exemplary Tory principles. "I have aimed," he stated in a manifesto which accompanied the programme, "at providing three hours of clean and wholesome entertainment, to put before you a bill of fare made up of the joys, the sorrows, the tears, the laughter, the soft romances, and the hard realities of our workaday existence, to restore its vitals to the theatre." What he succeeded in providing was laughter—an irreverent mirth quite alien to his intention. There could be no better illustration of the profound change in the theatre public's attitude to an essentially naïve play than its reaction to the serious effort of an old man to infect young Britons with the honest and simple emotionalism of his nonage. How far he had lost touch with the modern age was already evident in his use of such forgotten words as 'palpitating' and 'wholesome.' Palpitation was as obsolete as the vapours; wholesomeness as out of date as Martin Tupper. *Young England* was true to the pattern of Victorian melodrama. The hero, a scoutmaster—a modern touch which enabled the author to end his play with the "extra pleasurable feature" of a grand rally of Boy Scouts and Girl Guides— unjustly accused of theft from the Scout funds entrusted to him, performed his good deed by using the money collected for his defence to buy up and destroy the cheque forged by the dissolute earl, his father, to pay off his gambling debts. What hope was there that an age almost indifferent to tales of Nazi concentration camps and the daily sight of war-cripples selling matches and Welsh miners singing in the streets would be stirred to the old Victorian indignation at this absurd story of fictional injustice and self-sacrifice? The performers, embarrassed by the play's ingenuousness, acted it shamefacedly, already expecting to read the notice of its closure as they came out of the stage door. To their immense surprise *Young England* was received with hysterical delight. The playwright's noblest platitudes were cheered with ribald and tumultuous derision. The play ran on for years, transferred from one theatre to another, acquiring as it went a following of *habitués* who gleefully shouted the actors' lines before they had time to speak them. *O tempora! O mores!*

This unvarying reception of *Young England* wherever it was played—and it was played only in 'popular' theatres

like the Victoria Palace and the Holborn Empire—made
plain the fact that the cinema had drained off the popular
element of the theatre-going public. In this way the films
were doing a service to the drama. Incidentally, they were
completing the work begun by the suppression of the pit by
killing the larger theatres. His Majesty's, the St James's,
Drury Lane, and the Coliseum became white elephants.
Moreover, the enormous rise in theatre rental, due to the
lucrative practice of sub- and sub-sub-letting by the lessees,
big fleas and little fleas who thus drew their profit from the
theatre without incurring the risk of putting on a play,
helped the trend towards little theatres where a homo-
genous but smaller public could be economically absorbed
in lesser drafts.

The advantage to managements of diminished overheads
was, however, to a great extent offset by the rise in actors'
salaries. For this the films were again responsible. The
'talkies' had by now got into their stride and were making
an ever-increasing demand on the stage-actor. The lure of
Hollywood had become a serious menace to the theatre.
For one thing the absorption of the actor's vitality by his
work in the film studio resulted in much dull and listless
acting on the stage. For another, if a management wished
to retain the services of an actor it had to put him under
contract, otherwise when it wanted him it was apt to find
that he was either occupied at Elstree or had emigrated to
California. It was becoming a serious problem to cast a
West End play. To the playwright a play accepted was
farther than ever from being a play produced. In this
unstable state of affairs in which very few managements
owned a theatre (as the old actor-managers had done) or
had players under long-term contract it was necessary in
order to produce a play to do three things: to obtain a
suitable theatre, to find the financial backing in the City,

and then to cast the play. By the time two of these problems appeared to have been provisionally solved, the delay
in solving the third often led to the breakdown of the whole
project. In the days of the actor-manager at least somebody
was keen about a new play, provided it had a good acting
part—namely, the actor-manager himself, who, however
uninterested he might be in the play for its own sake, at any
rate saw it a vehicle for his own personality. Now nobody
was keen; keen enough, that is, not to be put off by difficulties, and the more important the principal part, the
harder it was to get the right actor for it. Sometimes in its
effort to overcome the three first essential preliminary
obstacles to immediate production the management would
be left with an empty theatre on its hands. Unable to carry
out or forced to postpone its original intention, it was thus
driven by expediency—it being cheaper to keep a theatre
open than to close it down—to put on a play in which it
had little faith, in the hope that with luck it might stop the
gap by running for a couple of weeks, only to find by the
end of that time that it had inexplicably caught on. These
plays usually belonged to what may perhaps be generically
termed the "drama of insignificance," a category which
found increasing favour in the 'thirties: plays with a minimum of plot, about very ordinary people, with little to
recommend them save a certain deftness of character drawing and a racy, colloquial dialogue. They were peeps at
insignificant pieces of life, authentic and precise, seen with
an observant and sentimental humour; sketches of medical
students preparing for their finals, of the 'crushes' and
rivalries of a provincial repertory company, of the effect of
spring on a commonplace family. They were the stuff of
the magazine story which editors say that only women can
write. They were restful little plays and they appealed
especially to women.

In the 'twenties D. H. Lawrence had asked these questions:

> Why are women so energetic?
> prancing their knees under their tiny skirts
> like war-horses; or war-ponies at least!
> Why are they so centrifugal?
> Why are they so bursting, flinging themselves about? . . .
> Why are they never happy to be still?
> Why did they cut off their long hair
> which they could comb by the hour in luxurious quiet?

In the 'thirties skirts began to lengthen. Women became more restful, more inclined to appreciate that seemingly impossible boon, luxurious quiet, if not for the purpose of combing their lengthening hair. Under the nerve-strain of living in a semi-lunatic world there were two alternatives: the one to go completely crazy, the other to cling to normalcy. The music-halls did the first, the theatre did the second. It was the men who packed the music-halls, the women who filled the theatres. Masculine and feminine tastes had parted company. But men thronged the promenade concerts and not only the music-halls; they discovered classical music as well as the Crazy Gang. H. M. Walbrook, a keen observer of the theatre for a quarter of a century, wrote this in 1937:

> I went one evening to see *Pride and Prejudice* at the St James's, and looking round at the pit in one of the intervals, saw that it was full, that the men in it numbered precisely five, and that not one of them looked younger than fifty. At a matinee of *Richard of Bordeaux* the writer and a playgoer from Liverpool were the only men in the crowded stalls, while the equally crowded pit contained row upon row of girls and women and not a sign anywhere of a masculine head and shoulders. Walking along Shaftesbury Avenue any evening when the pit and gallery queues are forming you will observe that they are almost entirely feminine. You will find young men in thousands listening to the music of Bach, Beethoven, and Brahms at the Queen's Hall.

The story of feminism, ending triumphantly in the en-
franchisement of women in 1918, of woman's hectic rivalry
with man in which she even flattened her figure in violation
of biological law, and of her return to restfulness and sanity,
does not strictly belong to a study of the theatre. It is
relevant in so far as it was the verdict of women which
increasingly determined the fate of a new play. It was
women who assured the success of *Richard of Bordeaux*, of
The Constant Nymph and *Escape me Never*, of *Autumn Crocus*
and *Quiet Wedding*. These were all written by women playwrights. Women had taken an equal place in the theatre
with man, not only as dramatists, but also as producers.
The following names may be mentioned: Auriol Lee, who
after a distinguished career as an actress turned producer,
beginning with *London Wall* and *The Wind and the Rain*
and becoming a specialist in Van Druten plays; Irene
Henschel, who produced *The Years Between* in 1926, *Eden
End* in 1934, and the Stratford-on-Avon production of
Twelfth Night in 1939; and Austrian-born Leontine Sagan,
who made her name with the production of the German
play *Children in Uniform* in 1934, and Ivor Novello's *Careless
Rapture* and *The Dancing Years*. The theatre of the second
half of the 'thirties was essentially a woman's theatre. Men
were too busy and too worried, life was too uneasy, for
them to have much interest in the theatre. Man is an idealist
or a scoffer. He needs a vision or a jest. Give him a poem
or a clown. If he went to the theatre of his own volition
in the harrassed days of never-ending crises, he went by
preference to the Mercury, or to a thriller or a farce. He
wanted, above all, to have a good laugh. "Laughter," said
a German, "is the English way of getting rid of something
which makes them uncomfortable." To him the theatre was
a form of escapism from the bedlam world around him: an
anæsthetic or a dream. Woman is different. She may be

romantic, but she is above all a realist. To her the theatre was not an escape but rather a tonic, a reassurance that the world was not as crazy or as desperate as it seemed. She did not care about plot or play-construction. What she most enjoyed was character and chatter. The play must be authentic and true to her experience, about people she could recognize, in whom she could see the resemblance to her relations and her neighbours. Let them prattle and bicker over some domestic difficulty with a nice love story as a secondary theme, and she was quite content. She came out of the theatre with her faith in human nature reaffirmed— for there was an underlying optimism in the drama of insignificance—and the feeling that her private little troubles were only the common lot.

If the playwright had written only to meet a calculated consumer-demand the stage would have been deluged with trivial conversation pieces. This kind of play was lively and humorous; it mirrored the pleasant surface of life. But it lacked art and imagination, whatever it is that "gives existence its surprise." Of the numerous tradesman play-wrights who were trying to make money out of the theatre, and their name was legion—Nigel Playfair declared in 1929 that he read four hundred plays a month—Hollywood fortunately seduced the more competent; the rest perished in the natural course of things. Luckily there were still writers who turned to the theatre, not as a coldly calculating gamble for affluence, but because they were bewitched by what J. B. Priestley called "the essential Theatre," because they came, as he says, "to see that the Theatre, though much of its appeal may be childish, is an institution that cannot safely be despised even by the philosopher." And so new dramatists emerged who brought back into the theatre imagination, philosophy and even poetry. The stage, long committed to a jejune realism, was enriched by the thought and technical experimentation of Priestley, James Bridie, T. S. Eliot, W. H. Auden, and Christopher Isherwood.

"Regret it as you may," Max Beerbohm wrote in 1900, "modern realism is the only direction in which our drama can really progress." Anyone who had watched the Continental stage throughout the 'twenties would have seen that there were many other directions open to it; but England has always been slow to profit by the experiments of foreigners. Now all of a sudden such plays as *The Sleeping Clergyman* and *The Black Eye, I Have Been Here Before* and *Music at Midnight, Murder in the Cathedral* and *Family Reunion, The Ascent of F6* and *The Dog beneath the Skin,* severally and almost simultaneously disproved the truth of Beerbohm's assertion. The theatre was out of its strait-jacket and re-equipped with brains; not just clever brains, but philosophic brains. Most interesting, and significant of an audience-change, was the return to poetry, or rather to stage-verse. The new poet-dramatists had learnt the lesson of the failure of the late Victorian poets when they turned to drama, the lesson put in a nutshell by Galsworthy when he warned John Drinkwater that "the shadow of Shakespeare is across the path of all who should attempt verse drama in these days." They wisely did not try to revive the glories of Elizabethan blank verse; instead they experimented, not wholly successfully, with a new form which embraced colloquialisms, holding itself in leash and even sinking deliberately into doggerel. These verse-plays achieved no wide or general popularity. They were too deeply influenced by German Expressionism, whether by direct imitation or because they were inspired by the same desire to interpret the inner life, the drama of the soul rather than the outward manifestations of ordinary experi-ence. They were rich in symbolism, and the British mind is never at home with symbols, preferring a simplified abstraction to a complicated riddle. They lacked the plain logic of cause and effect on which the theatre public had been trained to insist. They did, however, attract a small, enthusiastic *coteric*, which formed a nucleus for the renascence of verse-drama. And they were indicative of a new impetus at a time when it seemed as if the dramatist was bogged in skin-deep realism. *Murder in the Cathedral* was an exception. It was not expressionist. It was a return to the mystery or pre-Elizabethan morality-play. It had a quite astonishing success with a mainly middle-class audience, the more amazing because this class had always fought shy of religious plays, only taking to its heart such patently tract plays as *The Passing of the Third Floor Back* and *The Servant in the House*, in which the intrusion of a supernatural person, a strange lodger in a boarding house or an Oriental butler in a family, obviously representing the Saviour, successively reformed the types of the seven deadly sins.

With the arrival of these new dramatists a gust of ozone swept through the theatre, dissipating its stale cigarette-smoke and its sherry-party fumes. Not only their verse but also their prose broke away from the vulgar, wise-crack badinage that had come to pass as dialogue in which courage was alluded to as "guts," any kind of unpleasantness as "lousy," and damned and blasted and Eliza Doolittle's once-shocking epithet, were the only adjectives. Priestley's consciously 'heightened speech,' his breakaway from 'the flavourless patter of modern realistic dialogue,' and Bridie's cerebral garrulity had literary form as well as substance. Besides, the education of the public ear by the radio was probably creating a demand for finer dialogue as well as for an improvement in stage-diction. And as there were new dramatists who could write dialogue worthy to be finely spoken, so there were new actors who could speak it.

The 'thirties discovered Laurence Olivier, Ralph Richardson, John Gielgud, Edith Evans, and Peggy Ashcroft. Wisely and with rare abnegation they showed their devotion to their art by voluntarily enlisting for a term in the service of Shakespeare in the one place in London where he was still revered, the Old Vic, where the players received a salary of three pounds. The story of Lilian Bayliss's desperate venture and of her inspiring personality, her prayer for good actors cheap and the great work of her associates, Robert Atkins, Harcourt Williams, and Tyrone Guthrie, has been sufficiently told. At a time when the attitude of most producers of Shakespeare when he was comparatively rarely performed was to look for a new angle, to freshen up the Bard by some startling novelty, such as Komisarjevsky's *Merchant of Venice*, suggestive of the *Boutique Fantasque*, Terence Gray's 'ragging' of the same play in the manner of the Soviet theatre, or more justifiable experiments in modern dress, the Old Vic, under Robert Atkins and Harcourt Williams, built up a new tradition of simplicity of production and reverence for the text which was eventually to make it almost a national theatre. The pageantry approach to Shakespeare fell into desuetude and William Poël, who celebrated his eightieth birthday in 1932, still presenting Elizabethan and Jacobean plays under spatial conditions similar to those of their original performance, lived to see his teaching vindicated. Atkins's productions at the Old Vic, said Ivor Brown, were "Poël popularized." It was his opinion that "it is probably true to say that the Old Vic under his direction became more truly Shakespearian in spirit than any regular professional theatre since the age of the poet himself."

On Shakespeare's birthday in 1932 the new Memorial Theatre was opened at Stratford-on-Avon, and the poet's birthplace, "the dirtiest village in England" at the time of the tercentenary high-jinks (banquet and *bal masqué*) held there in a temporary pavilion in 1864, and neglected till the opening of the first Memorial Theatre in 1879, became increasingly a place of pilgrimage. This first Memorial Theatre, built by the almost unaided efforts of Charles Flower, a prominent local resident, who presented the site and bore much of the cost of its erection, was sneered at as "a theatre being built by the nobodies for the nobodies," and after its completion derided as a "bogus, half-timbered, fretted, and fretful affair," was burnt to the ground in 1926, a year after the granting of a royal charter. In fact it was a pleasant and comfortable theatre, and, with its seating accommodation for eight hundred people, adequately served its purpose to provide for a few weeks a home for an annual birthday festival. For almost thirty-five years— with one short interval—this was undertaken by F. R. Benson, whose Shakespearian company proved such a valuable training school for the London stage. The money for the new Memorial Theatre, sneered at this time as "a Soviet barracks," was raised by the *Daily Telegraph*, half in America to England's shame, but with the happy result that Stratford thus became an international Mecca, and in 1933 a six months' festival was instituted. Under the post-war direction of Sir Barry Jackson, with a policy of having a separate producer for each of the eight plays of the season's repertoire, the Memorial Theatre has, with the Old Vic, removed the long-deserved stigma that England neglects its greatest dramatist.

X

THE SUN GOES IN AND COMES OUT AGAIN

The Nineteen-forties

IN August 1914 the lights were metaphorically extinguished over Europe. September 1939 plunged England literally into darkness. The theatres were officially closed. The vestal fire of the drama was nevertheless kept burning by Donald Wolfitt, who offered the theatre-hungry lunch-time Shakespeare at the Strand. Meanwhile the Government, which had made no serious effort to provide proper air-raid shelters for its citizens, could no longer insist on its now seemingly needless precautionary ban on their enjoyment, and the theatres were reopened with a consequent boom; and as always happens in boom periods in the theatre speculative managements busily set about their customary policy of catering for the feeble-minded. Before the theatre, however, had time to produce another *Chu-Chin-Chow* the war began in earnest. The Battle of Britain snuffed its brief candle altogether. Alone the little Windmill Theatre braved the terrors of the Blitz, directing the appeal of its non-stop revues to the Anglo–Saxon's naïve and adolescent confusion of the erotic and the æsthetic, a confusion which has preserved his innocence about as often as it has landed him in trouble.

With the passing of the incessant menace from the skies the theatres again reopened one by one. London, more proud of its sense of humour than of its courage, sought its habitual relief from nervous strain in laughter. Two farces dominated the theatre during the latter part of the war: Noel Coward's *Blithe Spirit* and the American thriller-fantasia *Arsenic and Old Lace*. In the first a ridiculous but desperately earnest medium surpasses her wildest hopes of spiritualistic achievement by conjuring up the departed spirit of a married man's first wife. In the second two charming lunatic old ladies poison a long succession of visitors from the most benevolent motives. The astonishing thing is that the subject of both of these plays, which caused merriment to thousands, was one of the greatest gravity: life after death and murder. "You could see the audience," wrote James Agate, reviewing the first performance of *Blithe Spirit*, "sit up in horror almost as great as that of a golf-crowd when the champion fluffs his ball into a bunker." Murder had long been so over-capitalized in the theatre that the stage-murderer had become almost as ridiculous as the transpontine villain. The thriller-farce was as natural an evolution as the modern 'guying' of melodrama. But the endless popularity of a play based on the ridicule of a belief held by very many, a belief which the cruel bereavements of war had made desirable or at least less subject to scepticism, is more difficult to explain. If sufficient answer is not to be found in Noel Coward's wit and dramatic skill, we may perhaps, find it in de Quincey's apology for the general gaiety of his famous essay *On Murder*: "The very essence of the extravagance, by suggesting continually the mere aeriality of the entire speculation, furnished the surest means of disenchanting him from the horror which might else gather upon his feelings." Or was it simply that the war had converted all life to farce and that there was nothing else to do but laugh at it?

With the end of the flying bomb menace in 1944, for the first time since the outbreak of war nearly all London's

forty theatres were playing to capacity. Glory returned to
the theatre in the same year when a reconstituted Old Vic
company, joined and headed by Laurence Olivier and Ralph
Richardson, opened at the New Theatre. This was the
nearest thing yet seen to that long-fought-for ideal of a
National Theatre: a theatre devoted to the presentation of
great drama with a company of such high repute that to
act in it, to produce, or to design for it, was the highest
honour to which a man or woman of the theatre could
aspire. It showed that a new age of great acting had dawned,
but, as in every period when the actor is in the ascendant,
it drew almost entirely upon the drama of the past. It failed
to acquire the status of a true National Theatre in that it
excluded the living dramatist. It did, however, accomplish
two very important things. It brought Shakespeare back
into his rightful place in the West End theatre, and it
attracted the young. Boys and girls who had never been
inside a playhouse were magnificently given the chance of
seeing the poet, whose plays they had mugged up labori-
ously for School Certificate examinations, performed
thrillingly and—perhaps for the first time—with due emphasis on the minor characters when it properly belonged
there. For Shakespeare's drama is not a vehicle for adver-
tising a star-actor, although it requires one. (In *Othello*,
for instance, the first act depends entirely on Brabantio and
to a lesser extent on the Duke of Venice. The second act
is Cassio's, and so forth.) Yet it was as a vehicle for the
advertisement either of a star actor or a popular producer
that the stage had generally exploited it for the best part of a
century. The great merit of the new Old Vic was that it
was not—to use the old Victorian term—a company of
"stars and sticks." To introduce the young to the fascination
of great drama was a badly needed service, for youth was
all too easily seduced by the tinsel of the cinema, and though

schools had come to recognize the educational value of the drama the London stage had done very little to abet them in their work.

Perhaps the temporary black-out of the theatre during the war had served a useful end. The young enthusiasts of the drama in the schools and the rapidly spreading amateur movement in the country—it was estimated that there were as many as 10,000 amateur dramatic societies scattered throughout the kingdom in 1939, 2500 of which were affiliated to the British Drama League—seldom had an opportunity to see a professional performance. They had perforce to keep their interest alive by drama study. Thus a freshly imaginative audience was created for the revival of the professional theatre, and the warmth of an unsophisticated emotional response restored to it. A new generation of theatre-fans was largely self-trained in the appreciation of the quickening suggestion of the theatre. In the scale of "fandom" it was only natural that the actor should take first place. The youthful queues that gathered matutinally to secure their seats for the New Theatre came primarily to see Ralph Richardson or Laurence Olivier, just as their fathers had gone to His Majesty's for the sake of Beerbohm Tree and their grandfathers to the Lyceum attracted by the fame of Henry Irving. No producer has ever been adored, and not since Shakespeare has any dramatist been worshipped this side of idolatry. The revelation of the new Old Vic company was that after a lengthy period in which the actor had been to a great extent overshadowed, first by the dramatist and then by the producer, the actor was again worthy of the greatest rôles in classic drama, and was enabled to appear in parts worthy of his talents.

A new generation of young actors also began its training when in 1947 the old war-battered theatre in the Waterloo Road was opened as an Old Vic theatre-school and in the same year the Young Vic company was launched at the Lyric, Hammersmith, to carry on the tradition of its parent institution.

At long last Matthew Arnold's appeal for the organization of the theatre was finding a response. This work was greatly helped by the newly constituted Arts Council, which had at its disposal a moderate grant from the Treasury with which it was able to subsidize provincial repertory and small touring companies. In 1948 it had thirty-one such companies working in association with it. This subsidy was very necessary to the maintenance of a high standard of drama because of the severe economic handicap imposed on the theatre of high ideals by the Entertainment Tax. This tax was first levied in 1916. In 1948 it accounted for four shillings and eightpence of every sixteen-shilling stall. In the year 1944–45 it netted the Government £3,820,000 from theatres and music halls alone. The Arts Council was empowered, in order to raise the level of the drama, to recommend for exemption from this tax such theatrical productions as it adjudged to be of cultural or educational value. But English legislation rarely succeeds in exactly achieving its purpose. In practice the Arts Council did not sponsor individual productions. Instead it took under its aegis such companies as qualified for assistance by pursuing a non-profit-making and cultural policy. As these companies, by reason of their being non-profit-making, were, *ipso facto*, exempt from taxation, they were not unnaturally tempted to try to compensate the financial losses they incurred from the presentation of cultural and educational plays by putting on plays of which the cultural or educational value was dubious. Nevertheless, the work of the company being protected as a whole, these plays also escaped the Entertainment Tax. The first instance of such an anomaly was a comedy, the theme of which was bigamy supposed to have been legalized by an imaginary Act of Parliament! In 1949 the apparently inexplicable tax-exemption of the two American successes *The Death of a Salesman* and *A Street-car named Desire* called attention to the viciousness of the sanction imposed by the tax on other theatres.

The Arts Council did much to further the cause of better drama. Its work was most valuable in helping to decentralize the theatre and to make the provincial theatre independent, a process essential to the encouragement of local, and especially dialect playwrights, and of those who aim at something higher than scoring a popular success in the only place where he can be assured of adequate reward, the West End of London. The blight of commercialism eternally withers the London stage, or rather the immense hazards of production force commercial management to adhere to a policy of artistic timidity which automatically shuts the door on imagination and experiment.

Often the commercial theatre has had its hand forced and its fare supplied to it, handed it 'on a plate,' by the little suburban club-theatres which multiplied after the war. In many cases these little theatres tended to be a clique speaking to a clique, dallying with "pretentious semi-rubbish," but on the whole they were daringly and justifiably enterprising. The age had become self-conscious in its groping towards a new stability. The theatre public showed an unprecedented readiness to face facts, even ugly facts. Plays based on fact, what the cinema calls "documentaries," enjoyed a surprising amount of success, and most of them emerged from the little theatres: plays on human cruelty, on the Borstal and the prison system, on juvenile delin-quency and artificial insemination, sober, purposeful plays which before the war would have emptied any theatre. No individual has given more help to the struggling serious drama than Queen Mary, for every sincere and thoughtful play could be assured of being honoured by a visit from Her Majesty.

The phrase "pretentious semi-rubbish," used to describe many of these small club-theatre experiments, is unkind. It is culled as typical of a certain critical attitude towards inexpert efforts of imaginative creation. It has always been hard in the English theatre for the playwright to say something worth while. The 'forties were sternly logical and factual, and if the playwright had anything to say it was incumbent on him to put his message into documentary form. Critics had no leniency for symbolism or mysticism, the temptation of the earnest dramatist who aspired to profundity. Symbolism, so precious to the German, is high-flown 'piffle' to the Englishman. Mysticism, though more congenial, is difficult to make sense of; and if it made sense it would not be mysticism. Where, then, was there a way for the poet-dramatist who was not content to thrust the mirror into the face of daily life, who wished to explore the greater mysteries of Life and Death,

> Trying to learn to use new words, and every attempt
> Is a wholly new start, and a different kind of failure
> Because one has only learnt to get the better of words
> For the thing one no longer has to say, or the way in which
> One is no longer disposed to say it?

Was there then no escape from the *cul de sac* of naturalism? Was there only the futility of trying to overleap the walls of convention that hemmed the creative dramatist in, those walls which Lord Dunsany and Gordon Bottomley had ineffectually striven to surmount? He could turn back and revive some forgotten ritual form: the mystery or the morality play, or yet again the masque. It was risky to squeeze the lemon of Expressionism unless he camouflaged its nature by calling it "comic strip."

The most remarkable phenomenon of the 'forties was the success of two plays by unknown authors which recklessly abandoned the restraints of realism: Ronald Duncan's *This Way to the Tomb* and Donagh MacDonagh's *Happy as Larry*. To these must be added two plays by already famous authors, T. S. Eliot's *Family Reunion* and Thornton Wilder's *The Skin of our Teeth*. The first three were produced originally by one of the tiny periphery theatres which had earned by consistent adherence to lofty artistic policy the right to call itself "the Most Distinguished of London's Little Theatres." It had only a seating accommodation of 140 stalls, but its history is worth recording as it illustrates the way in which small esoteric audiences of Art-for-Art's-sakers were growing up. This particular audience was built up by Ashley Dukes, one of those selfless and faithful servants of the essential theatre, best known to the general public as the author of that exquisite piece of *marivaudage, The Man with a Load of Mischief.* He opened his little theatre in Ladbroke Road, and showed his hatred for every sort of convention, as well as the influence of Expressionism by calling it *the nameless theatre* (without capital letters) and announcing the presentation of a modern play in eleven scenes. The names of the author and the players were not disclosed; nor was the title of the play. These, it was promised, would be announced from the stage in the interval every Monday night. This idea was not entirely new. William Poël had kept his company anonymous with the Elizabethan Stage Society in 1898 for the reason that it was easier to appreciate the original merit of performances without the glamour of names. The extension of this anonymity to the author was perhaps an attempt to bewilder the dramatic critics, already astray in geographical *terra incognita* and solaced only by the possibility of obtaining at the bar an excellent port at sixpence and Napoleon

brandy at a half-crown a glass. If so, Dukes was only doing
what Shaw had done with *Fanny's First Play*, in which he
made one of them say: "You don't expect me to know what
to say about a play when I don't know who the author is,
do you?"

This jape, however, lasted only for a few months. In the
same year the theatre was christened the Mercury. "We
have ceased to be nameless," said its manifesto, "let us try
to be ageless." It opened under its new name with an
adaptation of Molière, followed by a translation of Henri
Becque's fifty-year-old *La Parisienne* and a Soviet Russian
farce. If it had done no more than continue along these
lines it would have become just another of London's little
highbrow theatres. But in 1935 Dukes announced a new
policy of isolationism: Plays by Poets. The first of these
was *Murder in the Cathedral*, produced by E. Martin Browne,
whose perception and sensitive direction have immensely
advanced the cause of modern poetic drama. After 250
performances it was transferred to the Duchess Theatre.
The successful transfer of *The Way to the Tomb* in 1945 and
of *Happy as Larry* in 1947 proved that there was a Third
Programme public for the theatre as well as for the radio;
that there was a growing interest in a modern poetic drama
which, as modern poetry had already done, jettisoned the
old ideas of versification, particularly in its rejection of
poetic diction in unpoetical circumstance. The mere fact
that Ronald Duncan, a Cornish farmer-poet, inspired by
Milton and Shelley instead of by the Elizabethans, could find
a hearing for a play written in the form of Masque and
Antimasque was a landmark of appreciative progress in a
theatre which had remained aloof from the introspective,
psycho-analytical, philosophical, and metaphysical dramatic
experiments of the Continent.

During the same period as the new poetic drama had

been developing in its shady suburban nook, what one may call the Light Programme theatre public had enthusiastically welcomed an 'about-turn' in the musical play. In the process of imitating the slick American farce-musical, librettists had shown themselves capable of concocting only second-hand silliness. The composers of light music turned out at best a few catchy, derivative tunes. They could reel these off like ribbon, the work of one composer being indistinguishable from that of another. English light music appeared at times to be in an interesting condition, but it seldom succeeded in being delivered of a melody. It was the librettist-composer Noel Coward who heralded the change with *Bitter Sweet* which, with its underlying nostalgia for the days when love was love and its tuneful music reverted at once to romance and melody. It was Ivor Novello who brought back the genuine romantic cajolery, the full glitter and glamour of the old Viennese operetta. With an unblushing emotional abandon and a perfectly straight face he gave his public 'the works.' *Glamorous Night*, produced in 1935 by Leontine Sagan, the first woman producer at Drury Lane, glutted the wildest feminine romanticism. With its Ruritanian splendours, its court ballroom and gypsy wedding, its spectacular sinking liner, and its story of a musical star and royal mistress in love with a handsome young Englishman, it had everything in it but the kitchen stove—and humour. But who would regret the absence of humour with so much to dazzle the eye and to delight the ear. *Glamorous Night* sounded the death-knell of the musical-comedy comedian and the tap dancer, and restored the singer to his and her rightful place in an entertainment labelled 'musical.' Here at last was a dramatic rival to the super-film. The libraries immediately took tickets for £40,000 which guaranteed a run of fifteen months and increased this sum by another £14,000 after it had been running for four months. From that moment the public never wavered in its allegiance to Novello's Lucullan recipe as one feast of tuneful glamour after another followed its prototype throughout the 'forties. Thus democracy satisfied the eternal hunger for romance which the legitimate stage denied it by its cynicism and matter-of-factness, just as the cafeteria was robbing it of the sense of aristocratic living provided by the Lyons' Corner House.

The English theatre had partitioned off its transparent moral, sentimental, and intellectual tendencies. With sentimentality rounded up in the corral of the glamorous musical the serious drama was in the main purged of this inveterate weakness. It was left to J. B. Priestley to do its moralizing and to James Bridie to provide its intellectual fireworks. These two skilful and versatile dramatists, each with his own conception of the educational mission of the theatre, continuously pricked the public's conscience or exercised its brains with tracts for the heart and for the head. Among the tribes into which the theatre public was by economic necessity splitting up, none were stronger than the tribe of Priestley and the tribe of Bridie. As money became shorter and living more expensive the habitual and omnivorous playgoer was driven to an eclecticism. The price of seats was a serious consideration, especially to the hard-hit middle class, which had been for so long the backbone of the theatre. Before laying out sixteen shillings or even seventeen and sixpence for a stall, it was necessary to pick one's play with circumspection. There were those who chose by reason of the cast and others because of the author, according to their ideas of entertainment. And though the general impoverishment diminished the bulk of those regular theatre-goers who never missed a new play, this was a good thing for the drama, for obviously those who were compelled by reasons of economy to eliminate opted for good acting in a good play. So, surprisingly when one considers the general level of popular plays, the outstanding successes of 1949 were three highly civilized plays: *Daphne Laureola*, *The Heiress*, and *The Lady's not for Burning*. The 1949 public's appreciation of their distinction would seem to reveal an unsuspected refinement of its palate. It must, however, be remarked that it swallowed with equal avidity the two American successes, *The Death of a Salesman* and *A Street-car named Desire*, plays coarse in language and violent in action and imbued with the pessimism that settled so curiously on the American post-war drama.

All these five plays were presented with the best acting and producing talent available. The names of the players and the high merit of their performances were alone enough to attract and hold the public. Yet the success of *Daphne Laureola* and *The Lady's not for Burning* must be given special consideration because by all normal standards these plays should have been caviare to the general. James Bridie, the author of the first, was a playwright who had hitherto exasperated the critics and delighted only a limited intelligentsia, and Christopher Fry, the author of the second, an almost unknown poet to the general theatre public.

When *The Lady's not for Burning* was given a West End production in May 1949—it had previously been played at the Arts Club Theatre the year before—the first-night audience actually cheered the poet. Almost overnight Fry's name was added, in the minds of the British public, to the company of the foremost playwrights of the day. Remember that for at least three-quarters of a century it had been positively asserted that poetic drama could never again have any popular appeal, an assertion which neither Stephen Phillips nor John Masefield nor John Drinkwater nor the Notting Hill school of verse dramatists had succeeded in effectively disproving. We must seek an explanation of this instanteous enthusiasm, this general recognition. Was it simply that the poet, instead of being self-conscious of the handicap of writing dramatic verse, and trying to castrate it by approximating it to colloquial speech, joyously delighted in the everlasting loveliness of words and thus intoxicated his audience with the same delight as Edmond Rostand in Paris did fifty-two years before? Is *The Lady's not for Burning* a fascinating anachronism like *Cyrano de Bergerac*? Or has its author gone some way to solve the toughest dramatic problem of the century? Has he, in one way, and James Bridie in another, unlocked the door against which so many modern dramatists have vainly beaten, the door which offers an escape from realism? Are these two plays no more than happy accidents or are they signposts for the drama of the future?

How does Fry's poetry differ from that written by his predecessors during this century? In the first place it is genuine dramatic poetry, neither lyrical excrescence nor half-ashamed verse studded with recondite metaphors and images. It is a zestful Elizabethan revelling in puns, alliterations, and conceits, yet not mere verbiage—but, like Rostand's, dramatic verse. His "April dance of words" both captivates the ear and lingers memorably. Whereas the nineteenth- and twentieth-century poetic dramatist has mostly striven after solemn beauties and grave felicities, his poetry is fraught with gladness, gaiety, and even flippancy. Like Bridie's prose, it goes hand in hand with laughter. Both Fry's poetry and Bridie's prose are verbally intoxicating and uninhibited. Already in *The Black Eye* Bridie hit on the truth that inebriety is the only valid reason for soliloquy, and in *Daphne Laureola* he has found an ebullient gaiety in that state of mellowness induced by alcohol. The two plays have broken out of the strait jacket of the conventionally constructed play, and their authors have not been over-troubled about plot, but have contented themselves with creating characters which are as alive and endearing as they are humorous and intriguing. For what are these plays about? The majority of their audiences when they left the theatre would have found it difficult to say precisely. What is important is that they did not care! Trained and accustomed always to seek a story and a meaning in a play, they went out exhilarated by two plays with the thinnest of plots and a meaning they would have been hard put to it to formulate.

"Plot," G.B.S., who did his best to dispense with it, once remarked, "has always been the curse of the serious theatre, and indeed of serious literature of any kind." One is tempted to ask whether the drama is at last to be freed from the necessity to tell a story. For all the other arts, including painting, and even music, had by nineteenth-century standards this constraint imposed on them. And if, like the novel, the drama is finding freedom from the necessity to tell a story what will replace it? Is laughter and verbal magic and character enough? There must clearly be always some minimum of plot, but is it not possible that these plays have shown the way to a new form of drama which has some affinity with music? Esmé Percy, the co-producer of *The Lady's not for Burning*, with a long experience of Shavian production behind him, has noted "the almost musical scoring of the play, its continuous variety of tempo, its essentially musical structure." The idea is not too fantastic. The term 'orchestration' was introduced into the critical vocabulary in connexion with the plays of Anton Chekhov. Young dramatists who followed in his wake gave their first plays musical titles: *Strange Orchestra* and *Musical Chairs*. That tireless experimenter, J. B. Priestley, followed a musical pattern of construction in *Music at Night*. The young post-war prodigy, Peter Ustinov, thinks dramatically and estimates critically in terms of music. Einstein once compared Shaw's plays in which the symphonic development is often clearly perceptible to anyone who takes the trouble to look for it to Mozart's music; and Shaw himself has written: "Do not suppose for a moment that I learnt my art from English men of letters. True, they showed me how to handle English words; but if I had known no more than that, my works would never have crossed the Channel. My masters were the masters of a universal language; they were, to go from summit to summit, Bach, Handel, Haydn, Mozart, Beethoven, and Wagner."

There is no need to labour the point. A play will always live and remain alive primarily by the opportunities it gives its actors. One may, however, hazard a guess that a new type of drama is evolving in which plot—as happened to melody in music, and story in the novel—is losing its paramount importance.

The renascence of the drama is always, like prosperity, round the corner. Throughout our century pessimists have bewailed the imminent demise of this chronic invalid, while rarely have optimists been unable to discover some portent of renewed vitality. Now, at the end our of century, the Government at last decided to be its nurse. The persistent and not too audible clamour, which had been raised for sixty years by those most concerned about its health, is soon to be satisfied. England is to have a National Theatre. Beyond the decision that when its erection is completed it shall be the inheritance of the then existing Old Vic company, no details as to its policy, management, or finance have been determined. But the mere establishment of a Comédie Anglaise will not bring in a golden age. This will depend largely on the actor and on the public; first, on the willingness of the leading actors and actresses of the day to restrict their independence and their earning capacity by tying themselves by contract for a period of years; and, secondly, on the insistence of the public that its repertory shall include a contemporary native drama which shall endeavour nobly to attack the universal problems of the times. Such a policy will provide a new incentive to the dramatist. Otherwise it will become little more than a metropolitan repertory theatre.

In the hundred years which have elapsed since Macready made his last attempt to save the stage from utter ignominy the actor has risen almost incredibly in status. A century ago the mummer was still—if not a rogue—a vagabond, a member of what was in the eyes of very many an ungodly profession, a social outcast living aloof from his fellow-men in a Bohemian quarantine, emerging only to entertain the public and then retiring to the segregation of his own fraternity. It was not till the eighteen-sixties that it was admitted that a man could be both an actor and a gentleman. It was not till the 'seventies that he need no longer apologize for his calling. When Gladstone stopped Henry Irving one day in Bond Street and introduced himself the encounter was symbolic of the admission of the actor to polite society, but in itself it was not unlike the meeting of Stanley and Livingstone, for, off the stage, Irving was as content to remain in his own island of Bohemia as Livingstone was to be lost in the dark interior of Africa. Irving welcomed his knighthood as an honour to the theatre, but although he permitted Society to invade his world of the Lyceum, he never sought to figure in the fashionable world. His successors, Tree and Alexander, moved serenely in Society. "They knew everybody and went everywhere," said Lady Tree of her husband, who even accepted as a compliment the charge of dilettantism. By that time acting was now no longer a suspect and mysterious vocation. The Profession had lost its capital letter; it was just a profession like any other, medicine or the law. Tree, perhaps, still trailed the romantic glamour of the artist; but Alexander seemed only incidentally an actor, for he did all the things that other professional and business men did, riding, shooting, playing golf, and serving on the London County Council. The Edwardian actor-manager was as much business man as artist. The actor after the war knew less of the business side of his profession but more of the complicated secrets of his art. The young beginner read and studied more deeply —there were more books for him to read—exploring theory instead of merely relying on natural talent and the hard lessons of experience. In the training of the repertory theatre, with its opportunities for the novice to turn his hand to anything, he learnt more about production, lighting, and *décor*, becoming in the process a jack of all theatre trades instead of simply an actor. On the one hand, this versatility has tended at times to make the clever young man of the theatre rather too eager to usurp all its specialized functions to himself, to be at once batsman, bowler, umpire, and the Pavilion cat. On the other hand, he has shown an unselfish willingness to submit to the discipline of team-work and the submersion of his personality. As a result, the art of acting has been raised to a higher general standard than ever before, and the greatest acting of the 'forties has reopened the door of magic.

Great changes have also taken place in the course of a hundred years in the status of the dramatist. In the eighteen-fifties, when Bulwer Lytton was still the most respected and popular dramatist, his annual income from the theatre was no bigger than that of a fashionable tailor's foreman or the combined stipends of two or three country parsons. From being an ill-paid hack adaptor and, if he had any pretensions to being a man of letters, contemptuous of his connexion with the theatre he rose, like the actor, to knighthood—and his profession to an esteem equal to that accorded to any other branch of literature. Financially the change has been stupendous. The introduction of the touring company and of the system of remuneration by royalties based on a percentage of the gross takings, the passing of the American copyright law, and finally the advent of the films have all increased the playwright's earning capacity, so that it is now possible for the author of a West End success to make a fortune. But the dramatist has not yet achieved the absolute freedom of the creative artist, for be it crude or cultural, moral or immoral, intellectual or imbecile, the theatre is, first and foremost, a place of amusement. To this fact the dramatist must yield. The list of established playwrights who have been mercilessly hissed when they have failed to please is a long one. There is no insurance in reputation won. On the Continent playwrights like Priestley, Emlyn Williams, and Terence Rattigan, who have proved their efficiency within the prevalent conventions, would be encouraged to spread their wings. In England managers are tradesmen, content with familiar goods under known labels. On only one occasion has the dramatist really achieved the first place in the theatre. This was a little-known incident that happened in 1916 when the actor who was to play the leading part in *Justice* happened to approach the front of the house and saw his own name displayed in very large letters on the billboards while the name of the author was inconspicuous. He immediately entered the managerial office and insisted on a reversal of the lettering. "If anyone wants to see this play," he said, "it is not because I am acting in it but because John Galsworthy wrote it." But that happened in America. The name of the actor was John Barrymore. "In France," W. S. Gilbert once said, "the dramatist has a right to claim success; in England he must beg for mercy."

Had Planché still been alive to-day to write a *Haymarket Autumn Meeting* in the fall of 1950 how would he have categorized our modern taste in entertainment? The favourite for the Big Race would unquestionably be Ballet Musical (by Oscar out of New York). "That can't be English," some one would remark. And the reply would be: "No, but it's the fashion," adding perhaps,

> The Lane is sure becoming a misnomer
> As local home for Broadway's *Oklahoma*;
> And *sine die* its revenues may be reckon'd
> The sinecure of Hammerstein the Second.

The second favourite must be Ruritanian Musical (of quite different breeding and owned by Mr Novello). Then would come the French filly Folies Bergères and the French-bred Latin Quarter. Then . . . but we need not labour the parallel with *Haymarket Spring Meeting*, 1855. One thing is patent. In the course of a century the English stage has only exchanged one master for another. It now borrows from Broadway instead of from the Boulevards. Superficially the panorama of the shows of 1950 does not indicate a noticeable rise in the level of intelligence . . . until we stop short at T. S. Eliot's *Cocktail Party*; but its London production was also anticipated by New York. Here they say that it was a great success over there, but here not one person in three can make head or tail of it. People write to the newspapers to say so—this public revelation of our theatrical reactions is a new feature of the age—and the producer writes back to declare that it is within the understanding of a child. In this he may be right, unless it be that he is more at home than the average man with symbolism, which seems to be gaining hold, as witness Tyrone Guthrie's *Top of the Ladder*, to mention the very latest of the descendants of Expressionism. It is not too fanciful to suggest that *The Cocktail Party* is merely *It's Never too Late to Mend* brought up to date, except that the parson has been super-seded by the psychiatrist and the sinner against society by the sinner against the higher ego as the material gaol has been exchanged for the triangular prison of ill-assorted matrimony. The fact that 200,000 people have seen it to date means nothing as an indication of public taste. We can no longer glean anything from mere numbers, for the theatre is affected by that extraordinary plenitude (another feature of the age)—that crowding and overcrowding which extends to beaches, hotels, restaurants, buses, parking places, and even post offices. With the few occasional exceptions, on the face of it the theatre does not appear to have greatly changed. Study the theatrical announce-ments. Is not this where we came in? The British public prefers musicals in the same way as gentlemen prefer blondes. There is truth in both these generalizations, but it is not the truth, the whole truth, and nothing but the truth.

How changed is the theatre public from that of a hundred years ago! Not in its composition but in its fundamental tastes. As one thumbs the scrapbook of a century and notes year after year the same inanities, the same expensive follies, the same preoccupation with blood and crime, one may be inclined to think that there is no way of educating it. Nothing will eradicate its elemental naïveté. It will never be entirely cured of sentimentality and sadism. The long line of spectacular plays and of plays of mawkish romantic-ism has culminated in the compound of the glittering and lavish musical. *The Vampire*, which in 1852 "supplied lovers of the revolting with three acts of murder," still has its abundant progeny. None the less, the public has pro-foundly altered in its attitude to the theatre. The idealism of its mentors has slowly effected this change. Time itself has furrowed its adolescent brow. Time has made it less superficially emotional, less responsive to heroism, less sympathetic to assertion. It has lost to a great extent the thrill of merely being in a theatre, the thrill that begins with the first tuning of the fiddle. It has lost the childish delight of listening to a story. It looks less for plot than argument. It can listen to talk without fidgeting for action. It is more insistent on logic and sound psychology. It is more able to face the truth, to bear the distressing spectacle of itself. It has been so persistently shocked that it can hear a spade called a bloody shovel without a qualm. It is more mentally alert, quicker to grasp a point. Its habit of going to the cinema in the middle of a picture has made it less necessary for the dramatist to dot his *i*'s and cross his *t*'s. Its habit of listening to the wireless has improved its ear, and after a temporary lapse into tolerance of slovenliness of speech it has become more sensitive to the beauty of language and pure delivery.

Financial impoverishment, the earlier opening of theatres, and food shortage have combined to make playgoing a more serious affair. The theatre has ceased to be a place where the well-fed and well-to-do may digest his dinner before it is time to have his supper. A comparatively empty stomach and a depleted purse have made the playgoer more exacting in his demand for full value for his money, for a good performance from the actor, and for some measure of intellectual or spiritual nourishment from the dramatist.

But a more far-reaching change is taking place than the redemption of the London stage from foolishness. Little theatres, youth and working-class group societies, are springing up all over England, as once did the chapels of Non-conformity, and the drama is by way of becoming an organized communal activity. There is promise that time may make true the dream of the theatre's visionaries and impossibilists, and it will take its proper place in the life of the nation as an auxiliary of the Church and the university.